The Message
of the
Accidental Mystic

The Message
of the
Accidental Mystic

Think about Becoming a Prepper

Imma Andkaer

iUniverse LLC
Bloomington

THE MESSAGE OF THE ACCIDENTAL MYSTIC
THINK ABOUT BECOMING A PREPPER

iUniverse books may be ordered through booksellers or by contacting:

iUniverse
1663 Liberty Drive
Bloomington, IN 47403
www.iuniverse.com
1-800-Authors (1-800-288-4677)

Because of the dynamic nature of the Internet, any web addresses or links contained in this book may have changed since publication and may no longer be valid. The views expressed in this work are solely those of the author and do not necessarily reflect the views of the publisher, and the publisher hereby disclaims any responsibility for them.

Any people depicted in stock imagery provided by Thinkstock are models, and such images are being used for illustrative purposes only.
Certain stock imagery © Thinkstock.

ISBN: 978-1-4917-1324-2 (sc)
ISBN: 978-1-4917-1323-5 (hc)
ISBN: 978-1-4917-1322-8 (e)

Library of Congress Control Number: 2013919690

Printed in the United States of America.

iUniverse rev. date: 11/05/2013

Dedicated to Michael, my husband.

Contents

Illustrations

Acknowledgements

To the Lord Jesus Christ, the Holy Spirit and my husband Michael.

Preface

This book is the compilation of notes that have been jotted down from the 1970's until now. My hope is, that even though I am not a writer, the message is understood in it's true aspect. The message is of the world just beyond our sight. We can become sensitive to this world. Energy creates the word. The word of decisive in-put of love and tranquility. What you think and believe, what you feel, all produces an energy of love or hate. It all can be seen. My husband and I accidentally entered into this unseen world.

We are all living in this place of light and love and energy, but we are too busy to rest and know it, to return to ourselves.

I will continue to keep currant, in logs, what is revealed by the "Touch". There will be drawings of what is meant to be revealed. All my notes, drawings and logs will be on my website.

Immaandkaer.com

Introduction

It was quite by accident in the 1970's that I learned that my husband, Michael, could see in the spirit. At first we did not know what it was or how it worked. But he recognized that it was similar to kirlian photography. If he closed his eyes after looking at a person, he could see their aura. Within each person's body he could see injury or disease. Even broken bones could be seen. Each person was affected by anger, love, hate, fear and so on. It all registered in different colors. The aura and the halo would change immediately. Anger would turn my whole chest area black. So I learned to get my temper under control. We kept notes and drawings as best we could. It was just learn as he looked.

So as the years went by and we raised our family, our attention was on them. Our children were all involved with sports, cheer leading, piano lessons and all the typical activities of a large family. The years flew by. We did not reveal Michael's gift of seeing. He did offer to help in a children's hospital and it was not received well. It was embarrassing. It did cause us to withdraw and remain secretive. Only a select few were seen by Michael. I would convince him to see someone and sometimes, the information he gave was not well received. It caused him to not want to see anyone.

We retired and sold our home and began a new phase of life, as oil painters. Busy and enjoying some success, though our time was very limited.

Then everything changed. I became ill. Michael would look at me, and he could see the large gray spot in my chest, in the area of the sternum. It was big! Like a big softball. But we thought cancer was purple and black. I was dying of cancer and did not know it. I had stage four cancer and had 18 months to live. I moved to Stanford Hospital after surgery and started treatments. I found my packed away notes and I began to write again.

I was spared by a miraculous touch from the Lord. Spared to write this book.

A few years passed, and quite unintentionally, Michael found that he could see letters when he touched my head with both hands.

Then words were seen. I kept writing as he told me what he saw. He told me I was to write my life. My journey of my life. The Lord Jesus called it my manifest. Michael was shown an image of me as a baby, toddler and young girl. I did not want to tell everything about my life. But repeatedly, Michael was shown what I should write.

If I am believed, then you will prepare your heart. If you trust that I have told the truth, you will turn toward the Lord, the Saviour, Jesus as we move into what will occur.

The "Touch" revealed that there would be a severe nuclear accident.

I asked if this was the "beginning of birth pains" of Matthew 24:8

The "Touch" revealed:

"COULD BE"

"THERE COULD BE MORE NUCLEAR ACCIDENTS"

"BUT ONE IN INDIA COULD BE MORE SEVERE"

"IT DEPENDS   IF MAN'S CAPABLE OF PREVENTING"

India could choose to repair its electrical infrastructure. If the next time their electrical system fails, could an accident happen? And is man capable of preventing nuclear accidents? I don't know.

"Free will" is revealed to Michael all the time.

The statement, "ONLY TIME WILL TELL", means that the future is flexible and not fixed. It is a constant set of choices that mankind is making. Free will is everything.

Michael touched my head and the "Touch" revealed:

"FEAR CONFUSION   LOVE   PREPARATION"

The meaning was fear in my childhood and my state of mind in confusion while maturing. The love was the healing love of God when I was saved.

But Michael and I did not understand preparation. So we talked it over and asked again what is the meaning of preparation? The "Touch" revealed:

"FEAR AND PREPARATION IN THE BOOK"

We were still confused. I asked if we were to be in preparation for problems? Maybe hard times are ahead? What are we to prepare for?

The answer is in my message to you.

"PREPARE"

Chapter One

The Beginning Experience of a Wounded Child

It must have been cold. Very cold in the winter time of early January of 1941. I was just twenty months old . This foreboding beginning could not have been altered. This fateful, ominous time could not be changed.

We lived on eleven acres in California and had a small farm.

My mother had just given birth to my younger sister, ten days earlier. The photos that I have of my mom, show a beautiful and affectionate mother. Holding me and playing with me.

When she gave birth to my older brother, nine years older than me, she was not to have any other children. She had gone into, temporary, deep psychotic, psychosis. Then came my older sister, by 4 years. Again, a temporary psychotic state. Then I came along. She was not as bad with my delivery and a shorter psychotic period. (I have found, 70 years later, that this was not true.)

She was very beautiful and had been a ballerina. She came from a large, early California, pioneer family. A Danish immigrant's family. Delicate and frail. A soft voice and quick wit. A bit of an artist and she played piano. So I believe that I really loved her. Bonded with her as completely as a baby can. The photos of her and me being silly and loving, portray it.

So when I was twenty months old, she gave birth to my younger sister. This time she didn't come back. She went into the deepest psychotic state and was institutionalized after ten days. I believe they did try to let her come home to be with the baby on a visit?. Perhaps after a few months? I remember the baby. I looked over the side of a cradle and saw her.

But I also remember two nurses coming into the house. There was a man too. He must have been a doctor. Mom was crying softly and they took her by the arms and led her away. I was helpless. I didn't even cry?

I feel this was a shock, or trauma for me.

(Now, after 71 years, I have learned the truth. My daughter's doctor acquired the file on my mother. It is at the end of this book. She came home at least 22 times for weekend visits between 1941 and 1943. She was allowed to be alone with us. She had gone mad and was a schizophrenic. I do know from aunts and other family members that I was found two or three times, unconscious under her or being squeezed tight by her.

My almost lifeless body was torn away from her on at least three occasions. My grandmother wrote the hospital, that she feared for our lives and our safety.)

I have no memory of the next year. My grand mother and grandfather took me. My little sister went to our maternal uncle and his wife. My older brother and sister stayed with my father.

My memories of my years with my grandma were loving and warm. She was a Danish power house. Secure, safe and I could sit on her lap anytime. She told me over and over again, that I was a cousin to the royal family. I didn't know what she meant, but she would dress me in long dresses and I would dance and dance. She treated me as though I was a princess. She curled my hair and dotted on me. Dresses and curls and ribbons and bows! I had dolls and a doll house and was always in dress up, play time.

I found her weeping one day. It frightened me and I begged to know what happened. She said her papers had all been burned, by accident. Everything was burned. She had been receiving dividends from Europe and needed her papers for identification. She cried for a long time. I tried to comfort her with a pillow.

On a visit to my aunt and uncle I do remember being very worried that grandma would leave me. I asked her to promise, she would never leave me. She promised. Then I asked her if, "Could I be sure to die before you, so I would not be without you?" She promised. Then she hugged me. I must have been almost four.

I did see my mother once when I was around four,—an overnight. She was on a visit and my sisters and brother were there. My mother was so beautiful and I just wanted to hear her speak.

2

As I remember, it was an uneventful visit. I went back to my grandma.

She did come to my grandma's house one time. My mother had run away! My grandma said she had to go back. I remember the words as though it was yesterday.

"You have to go back!" Grandma said.

It must have killed my Grandma to do it. This was her favorite child that she was sending away. I just looked on. My mother held my gaze and gently smiled at me. I said nothing. I just looked at her. I stood frozen! Helpless to it all. Helpless.

My grandma and grandpa were my parents. They were my everything. I was tucked in at night and secure. All was well.

They would take me to see my mother, perhaps twice a year. The buildings were huge and I thought it was a castle! We would go on a picnic or out to a country, outdoor garden, restaurant. It was enchanting to be with her. She was so beautiful and her voice was soft, like a whisper. Black hair and dark, dark eyes. She would always give me a little present of some kind. Some coins or some ribbons. I cherished them and held them close to me. Then I would say "good bye" to her. I never cried. Strange that I never cried.

Chapter Two

Early Years and First Marriage

I think I had the measles. I was tucked in and cozy and warm. The sun was up, but I was still in bed. Grandma had taken my temp. She was standing at the foot of my bed. I was almost five years old. I looked up and a strange man was standing over me. Grandma started screaming! Crying and screaming and yelling. The man grabbed me and started out the door. Grandma chased us. Screaming and screaming! I was terrified. But she couldn't get to me. I was helpless. There were two other men in the car. They put me in the car and I could see her. She was running after the car and screaming!

I said to myself, "I am too afraid. I can not go through this. I am going away." —I went away. It was the only way to survive and I must have known this as a child. I split away. I was gone to somewhere else? I didn't cry.

The man was my father. The others were my paternal grand father and my uncle.

I do not have any memory of the next few weeks. The first time my memories started again was when a little tiny girl, with big dark eyes, walked into the room. She was so tiny and frightened. She was crying! I went to her rescue. I ran to her! It was my little sister. I was going to be OK now, I thought. I will take care of her. We stuck together like glue. We slept together, ate together and played and played. She told me she heard bad things about our brother. I didn't know what they could be. But I was soon to find out.

My father was a gambler and was gone a lot on the weekends drinking and gambling. We were OK alone, although we would get very frightened when my brother would terrorize us at night. He would go outside and pretend to be a robber and tap on the windows in the dark! Or say he saw someone in the yard! He was cruel and mean.

When I was about five, I was left alone one day with my brother. I was out in the yard, playing. I could hear him calling me. But I stayed hidden. I was fearful and shaking. He was getting closer. He was getting closer and closer to me as I stayed still, and hidden! I was hardly breathing!

He yelled, "If you don't come out, I am going to kill you when I find you. And I will find you!"

Well, I wanted to live. I didn't want him to kill me. I wanted to live. I made the choice, I stood up and thought, he won't kill me now. But he took my hand and said "come with me". I was in such terror that I said to myself "I have to go away now".—I went away.

When it was over my brother said to me, "If you tell anyone what happened to you, I will kill everyone you love. Everyone! I will kill them all. Then I will kill you!".

—I wanted to live. I loved my little sister now! I wanted to love. I froze inside. I felt paralyzed. I told no one. I bore it alone. It was gone from me. Just gone. And part of me was gone again. I was sad. But I didn't allow myself to cry.

Life went on. We had a small farm with cows, chickens, rabbits and dogs and cats. After a few months, my father asked, "would you like to see grandma?" I said "no". I couldn't bear to see her. That person went somewhere? I could not reach her and I did not want to feel anything. I needed to harden myself and take care of myself. I wanted to survive! I wanted to live.

I started school and was always the best, the fastest, the smartest. I was very dirty from not being washed and bathed. But somehow I knew I was capable of being accepted by my playmates at school. I knew I was pretty. I was so capable of anything I attempted to do! My older cousin was staying at my Grandma's and she would wash me in the rest room before school. I was driven to compete and come out first! Just competitive in every move, as I wanted to survive everything.

With no mother or supervision, we just played and got to roam the hills and country side. I found that if I ran in the hills and fields, until I dropped in pain, some of the tortured feelings inside me would ease. We could run in the hills for miles and miles. No one was there, except for an occasional cow herder on horseback. Our swimming pool was huge cow troughs! You just didn't put your nose under water!

I loved nature and was a natural artist. I drew everything. I went to church with any girlfriends that would take me along. I knew about Jesus and God the Father. I liked that Jesus was the Son of God. We were catholic and went to church on holidays.

The catholic nuns would bring us shoes. They all knew we were left alone and they were kind. The shoes were not pretty shoes, but we wore them. We were a rag-a-muffin lot. Our bath water had to be heated on a wood stove. So a bath was quite a project. You would have to hurry with the pots from the stove and run to the tub! My little sister and I did the laundry. Old machine and wrung through the wringer. Then put on the clothes line.

We did all the housework. We didn't know we were poor. Friends would share their school lunches with me if I didn't have anything to eat. We were taught what Indian lettuce was. We would pick it in the woods and run home and put mayonnaise on it. Yummy! I have kept in Touch with all my classmates. I love them. I guess they became my family. I have wondered for a lifetime why I loved them so?? —I bonded, as I would have, with a family.

When I was nine, my grandma and grandpa came to live with us! It was like heaven! We were bathed and clean! The house was overhauled! What order and grand meals! Everything was wonderful. She was strict! One afternoon I was way up on a hillside playing and I heard her call.

"Mary Imma! Come now, for dinner!"

And even though I wanted to keep playing, I started down the hill. She saw me coming and called, "Do not dawdle! Run!"

And I replied, "I would like to see you run down this hill!"

I got down the hill and she calmly put a bar of soap in my mouth and scrubbed every spot in my mouth! And my teeth! I can still taste it!

A few days later she was sitting at the sewing machine and I heard her say to herself, "I'd like to see you run down this hill".

I felt bad for what I had said and if I had upset her. But I was powerful now and ready to stand alone.

Within the week, I woke early one morning and went in to kiss her, as I always did, before she woke up. But she was cold and her lips were blue! I started yelling at her! Then screaming and running! I curled up in a little ball and just screamed!

My dad yelled, "Don't be upset! I just heard Grandma call for you!"

And so I thought there was hope! Hope that everything was OK!? I ran back to her with hope! I bent over her and called to her to come back to me! "Come back to me"!

7

She had promised not to leave me. But she was gone. Hope was gone.

The relatives came quickly. Her sons and my aunt. They took her jewels and anything they wanted from the house. They went through everything. They took dishes and paintings from the walls. Most of the items were my mothers. But they took whatever they wanted! (Fifty years later, an aunt gave me back my Grandma's watch. She said she was sorry)

At the funeral they made me go and look at her in the casket. I didn't want to. But they made me. She was gone. I was almost ten years old now.

Back at school my little friends had heard what happened to my Grandma. They were all kind to me. School and my teachers were my refuge. My safe place in the storm. I excelled and fought to be the first in everything. In all my years, in this small little town, no one ever mentioned my mother. No one ever made fun of me. No one ever laughed behind my back. Even though I was poor and didn't know it and my mother was ill, my little friends didn't hurt me. I have kept in Touch with almost all of them.

So grammar school was over and it was summer vacation. Getting ready for freshman year in High School! All grown up and just turned thirteen. Always allowed to run. No one was at home now. My brother had joined the service. My older sister married and younger sister moved in with a family of her best girlfriend. My father was gone gambling and different jobs that took him away. There was no food or money most of the time. I found white cake flour in the cupboard. Mixed it with water and I got it down. Since I was alone, I could walk to my girlfriends, down the road a mile, and spend the night with her. It was a hot summer night. There were girls and guys and a party was going on when I reached her house. A couple of kids with cars. Everyone was jumping in cars and going to go somewhere. I jumped in a car too. I knew the driver, he was nice and a little older. A few boys that my sister went to school with. And his brother that went to school with my brother. Everyone was laughing. They stopped and got some beer to drink. A boy that I didn't know tried to kiss me and I pushed him back and away from me. I guess it made him mad and I was unaware of his anger.

They drove to an isolated area and got out of the car. It was a bright moonlit night. We were all laughing and walking on the road. The guys said lets go back to the car and go back to town. I was following behind and walking back toward the car. I took a great blow to my back and went down. The wind knocked out of me. A boy I knew was holding my head and shoulders down. The boy I had pushed away, was pulling my jeans down. I kept saying "Wait a minute! Wait a minute!" In a split second I was raped. I was horrified and in terror. I pulled my jeans up. I thought they were going to kill me.

So I ran and ran into the woods. I didn't know if I should stop and hide because my breath was so loud. I was like a little rabbit hiding. Running and then stopping and hiding. I couldn't breathe from terror. My heart was pounding so loud that I thought they could hear it! They will find Me! They were yelling my name and trying to find me!

8

They are going to kill me. So I curled up in a little ball to stop the sound of my loud breath! Stop the sound of my beating heart. The boom from my heart must be heard by them!

And then one of them found me. He reached down and said "You are not going to be hurt. I will watch over you. Come with me and we will take you home".

It was his younger brother that had hit me from behind and dropped me and held me down. I did not speak. They took me home.

Then I was taken to a hospital. It made the newspapers. Not my name, but everyone knew. It went to trial. I remember asking God if I could die? It would be merciful to let me die. It was horrible. To testify on the stand about what happened to me was shattering! Then it was over.

But I didn't die. I went on to high school. One of my brothers buddies, Jake, from the Service, came home with him on leave. I didn't have a good feeling about him. But he seemed nice and he was friendly with everyone. He had just started a job on the police force. He knew about the trial and the case.

My older sister began to baby sit for Jake and his wife.

I always remained friends with Jake, through high school. He was ten years older and it would seem he was too mature to be around my high school friends and kids. However, in my senior year we began to date.

We drove to Los Angeles and stayed with his family. They were wonderful. I liked all his extended family! We got engaged around my graduation time.

He did have a huge temper! But he would calm down quickly and always assure me that he was just fine. I trusted him.

I wanted to go away to business school in San Francisco. I gave him his ring back. I broke off the engagement and he was furious!

I did go away to school for a year. My best friend, Joan, from high school, moved in with me in a one room, tiny, apartment. We had a bed that came down from the wall! With a tiny kitchen nook, that only one person could fit in at a time. In the heart of the Tenderloin! We had only pennies to live on. We made potato and onion soup with a lot of spices and lived on it for days at a time. But it was just wonderful to live in San Francisco! On the corner of Leavenworth and O'Farrell Streets. The heart of the tenderloin! The land lady was old, old and adored us! She would invite us country bumpkins over for strong Turkish coffee! So strong you could hardly drink it! I completed the business school and was very happy in San Francisco.

9

We invited Joan's family over and they were shocked at the location and surroundings! Even though we found it just fine, they moved us out the next day. They moved us to Pacific Heights. Into a tiny apartment! Students from the business school introduced me to some of their friends. I was dating a little. But no one special. The school placed me in a good job with an insurance company. I would visit my family and relatives every month or so by greyhound bus.

My roommate Joan, decided to move in with her boyfriend. So I had to move into a smaller studio, in the same building. But it was lonely without her.

My sister got in Touch with me and said that Jake had visited our family, from Los Angeles. He was trying to find me. Then within a few days, I saw an ad in the personals. In the S. F. Examiner! It said "Imma, get in Touch with me. Only me! Jake"

I thought this must be very important! Serious! For him to drive all the way from southern California to find me! And now an ad in the newspaper?

So I decided to see what he wanted. And to fly down to see his Mom and family would be fun.

I arrived in Los Angeles and called his Mom to say I had arrived. And where would I find Jake?

She was shocked to hear from me! And gave me his phone number.

I reached him and he said, "I told you to only contact me!" He sounded upset!

He gave me his address and I took a cab to the house. When I arrived he explained that he had been living with someone. Not married, but his mother knew he was living with someone! They had separated. She was gone. She had moved to Arizona with two small baby boys! This was the same girl that he was seeing when I was in High School!

Oh boy, I was in trouble! Jake convinced me that we should be together. He would quit his job, immediately, and we would drive back to San Francisco and I would keep my job.

OK. That sounds OK? But he had to give two weeks notice! I did not want to loose my job. So I called my employer and said I was getting married! They gave me the time off.

As we drove up the west coast, I stopped to call my father and tell him I was getting married. He said, "to who"!?

I said, "Jake"—He started sobbing! He begged me not to. I was so frightened and I assured him I would be OK. Not to worry!

We found a small apartment and I saved my job.

We went to Reno and got married over a weekend. I cried quietly during the ceremony? My life was spinning out of control! And at a lightning pace!!

I cooked and cleaned and went to work. We were comfortable in our little apartment. I fell in love with my husband!

But he was unhappy with me! He was critical and insanely jealous. I was timed where ever I went or walked.

I got pregnant and he seemed happy about it. He got a different job, right next to our apartment and we were both able to walk to work. I really liked his boss and his wife. I would help out sometimes serving crab cioppino at lunch, when I was not working. It was fun and I knew everyone.

Someone had spilled liquid on the floor. I did not see the spot. I had high heels on and took a terrible fall on my backside and butt. I was well over five months pregnant at the time of the fall. Within hours my water broke and I was hospitalized.

After two days, of attempts to keep me out of labor, I delivered a baby boy that died within minutes.

I was devastated. Everyone thought I should go back to work immediately for my mental health. I did return to work. After a week, I became ill. It was found that gangrene had set in and I needed a D & C. So back to the hospital I went.

The last thing I remembered was the face of my anesthesiologist and my doctor. I have recently learned that not only do I go into shock with iodine, but also with many anesthetics. Well, I died.

I went into the outer space. Far out into the universe. But it was in a state of separation from God. Separation from my real self! It was as though I was in a circular revolution, would connect with my self and then go into separation again. But it was for eternity! Separation eternally! I was in Hell. I knew it was my death state. I knew I was off into anguish! Forever! But then things started speeding up. I was going back toward earth. I could hear a great roar. The sound that was earth! It was louder and louder and then faster and faster!! I was back in my body. As soon as I was conscious, I tried to tell my doctor!

"I died", I screamed at him! But he turned away and walked out the door.

There after, he would not discuss it with me. He did not want to hear anything about it.

11

Friends brought me home from the hospital. My husband was gone, with friends for a few days. I could not walk. So I crawled for water and then got back into bed. Within a few days I was back on my feet. Then Jake came home.

He sat down across from me, looked me straight in the eyes and said, "If you say one word about my being gone, we are finished. I will leave you"!

I did not have any strength to fight him. He made it as though I had done something wrong. That I should be silent. I was silent.

I returned to work and our life settled down into our routine of work. I made a best friend at work. A married girl with a baby boy. We would go out to lunch and I met her family and friends. She was nice and I confided in her about my unstable marriage and his temper. She was sympathetic and wanted to know more. All in confidence, of course. Because of my job at the ambulance and medical dispatch, the rumors were flying! I didn't believe any of the rumors, that he was cheating!

Then one evening, as I walked home from work, I saw our car driving toward me. But there was a girl sitting right next to him! As they came closer, Jake saw me and pushed the girl, downward and away, and sped past me. I did not see who the girl was. Later that night he assured me that I was crazy and it was not him!

OK? But I was now on the lookout!

He said he wanted a more luxurious apartment so that he could entertain all his very influential friends! The DA, nightclub owners and friends. So we entertained and partied.

I was working and would walk home in the evening. It was at least eight blocks and some uphill! One night he was waiting for me, furious! He said I was late.

I said, "I just stopped to buy a pack of cigarettes at the diner"!

He grabbed my arm and pulled me down to the street! He said,

"We are going to time you and they better recognize you."

So he drug me, running and pulling me in my high heeled shoes! Thank God everyone in the diner recognized me and assured him that I did, indeed, buy cigarettes! Again, he cried and begged forgiveness! And I forgave him.

But he started not coming home, often. I found a phone number and around 4 am I dialed it. A young girl answered and I asked to talk to Jake. He got on the phone and tried to talk with an Italian accent. What a dummy! I had heard that at parties for years.

12

I said, "I know it's you Jake".

I left and filed for divorce. I moved in with a girlfriend. I continued to work and actually had my wages attached for one of his debts! But I had my friends and family. Especially Dorothy, my best and closest confidant.

But Jake was relentless in pursuit of reconciling. He felt that if we moved to a new location he could make a break with the past and stop drinking. He would stop drinking and we could start dating! Just give him a chance.

And so, after a time, we found a little cottage and both moved back in together. Once settled in, he said in low tones, "No one ever leaves me!" —well, I thought, that might be good! Perhaps he means it will work this time?

After a few smooth months, I found I was pregnant again. This time he was very happy with the idea! He felt that if we started to go to church, perhaps he could get help? He would try to change! And so we began to attend a small Episcopal Church. He had known the priest for many, many years. I was happy to attend church and felt we were on the right path! Jake wanted me to be baptized and set it all in motion. And so I was baptized, Jake was my God-father and my hopes were high!

But within a short period of time, perhaps just weeks, he was growing agitated again. I decided to go to a psychiatrist, secretly. My visits with the doctor were within walking distance and I began therapy.

After a few weeks, he said to me,

"You had a bad father image. I have never advised a person as I am going to advise you now! You have made a terrible mistake. You are in trouble. Leave him! There is nothing you can do to fix this. Get a divorce! But leave him"!

I left his office and just walked and walked. And I did not want to leave. But as the next few weeks went by, I could see that Jake was getting worse and worse.

We came home late one evening, after dinner out with friends. He had a few drinks. I got out the passenger side and was behind the car, thinking he would turn off the engine. But the car raced back at me and I jumped out of the way. He professed how sorry he was and that he didn't see me. I knew I was finished with him. But I said nothing.

The next day I came home early from work. I talked to our landlady. She lived within a few feet of our cottage. I explained to her that I must leave. Right now, this minute. That the baby, and my life, depended on my leaving immediately. We would surely die. Even if it was just by an accident. She told me to leave. "Now"!

13

I packed just my clothes and personal items and walked away. I took a bus to my sister's. I could keep my job and get to work by bus.

It was around eight in the evening that Jake broke into the house. I had only told my girlfriend, Dorothy, where I was going? But here he was! My sister ran next door to the police department! Two policemen came in and got control of him. They convinced him to leave and that a domestic problem like this could be settled in another way. He left and I felt no immediate threat.

The next morning I walked out the front door to catch a bus for work. He was there, hiding and threw me in the car! Next door to the police department! He was screaming and yelling!

I didn't say a word. I said to God, silently, "let me live. Let the baby live".

We made it back to the cottage and Jake was calming down. We were upstairs and I assured him I would talk to him after work. I needed to go to work and keep my job. I was ready to leave and started down the staircase.

By now I knew to say and do anything to save myself and the baby. Of course I forgave him!

I would see him after work, I said. And I left and went to work. All the while confiding again in my very good friend, Dorothy.

I left work early and found a studio room with a kitchenette. Took my few belongings and moved in. Walked to work and had a few peaceful days. No one knew where I lived. Except my best friend Dorothy.

The evening of the third day, he broke in. By now I was big! Almost eight months along.

I did not move. Helpless. I asked God if I could live and have the baby. I waited. It took hours. He began to breakdown. He cried and cried and asked for forgiveness. Of course I forgave! He left and said we would talk tomorrow night. That gave me another day!

I went to work early, got off early. Saw an ad in the newspaper for a share rental with two other girls. I begged and cried to let them just meet me, before they said no. I told them the truth and they let me move in. I moved within minutes.

I would file for divorce after the baby was born.

I asked for time off at work as my time drew close. The girls had a shower for me and I was feeling much better. I saw our car near my work and went in to the bar and restaurant to see if Jake was there? He was! And sitting on his lap, was my best friend, Dorothy. She was the one in the car. She was the one that was telling him each place I moved! She was the one putting my life in danger! They were together all this time!

I just walked away. What a dummy I was. All the times I told her where I was and where I was going. She was alerting him. What a dummy!

And we worked together! I told my supervisor and the owner of the ambulance company. They separated us by shifts.

The girls I moved in with were excited about the baby. The flat was huge and very nice. My aunt and uncle came to visit. I was comfortable. I was almost twenty-one. It was 1960!

It was a race to the hospital! My roommate's boyfriend Michael was there to care for me and took me to the hospital. I almost did not make it! In the hall and then into the delivery room and within 19 minutes the baby was born!

I said, "Is it a girl or a boy"?.

My doctor said, "It's neither! You have a tiger on your hands!"

A beautiful, healthy, alert and perfect baby boy!

After a few weeks I went to stay with my sister. I needed to go back to work and she would watch the baby. I took the long ride, by bus, to work. I was angry that I had to leave the baby! I was frightened to leave him, even though I did trust my sister.

At work I found my best friend, Dorothy, had her hours changed and was working right there along side of me! While she was living with my ex-husband! The urge to choke and strangle her was overwhelming! So I got up and walked away from my job. I didn't go back.

My first job in San Francisco hired me back. I found child care just up the street from the flat that I shared with two roommates. It was a long day and a long commute.

I didn't make enough money to get by and pay for child care. I needed some help. So I went to the county offices and asked for help to find Jake and enforce the decree of support. I pressed the DA or his assistant, for help!

He said, "Go and get county aid".

I said, "No! I have a good job. I just need help!"

He yelled at me, "What do you want me to do? Give it to you out of my own pocket?" He was yelling at me! I just walked out.

But at lunch, in San Francisco, I spotted my ex and followed him to his office. He was actually working near my job. I confronted him! Boy was he shocked. Later I gave his whereabouts to the county offices.

He was angry about child support! More threats. I quit my job and stayed home with the baby. The county could now chase him down!

I received about $98 dollars a month. But I had medical and food stamps. I could work part time a little and a percentage would be taken out of my allowance. At least I wasn't having contact with my ex.

My divorce was final and the girls that I lived with started introducing me to friends of friends, so I would get out of the house. I met and started dating a friend of my roommates boyfriend, Morris. Morris was a gentle and kind person. He had recently been discharged from the service and took me to meet his family. My roommate was dating Michael. Michael was the best person I had ever met. In my young, silly and immature state, I still knew. He would always be the finest person I would ever know. He helped me with the baby and would take me shopping. We baptised the baby and Michael became his Godfather.

It was fun with the girls, but we were up two flights of stairs. A straight run up and down. Jimmy was starting to crawl and had almost gotten near the top of the stair case! I decided to move closer to my family. So I found a studio apartment by the time he was walking. Morris would take Jimmy and me out. He was good with Jimmy, but he started being too jealous.

I would go out on the weekends with my large family group and he would show up! I didn't like it! Sometimes he would be parked outside my apartment all night! I was just getting over the trauma of my husband and now I was having more problems. So I broke off any contact with Morris and ended it. He almost got killed as he drove home that night. He must have been driving too fast on the freeway and lost control. He rolled over and over and totaled the car. But it was a big, older, Chrysler and he did not get hurt.

The summers were fun with Jimmy. He loved the pool at the apartments! We were tan and healthy. I could still work part time and get by.

I wanted to meet someone that cared. Someone to fall in love with again. I did not like being alone. I wanted to be married. Jimmy needed a father. My brother in law "Bill" would come over and help me put Jimmy to sleep. Jimmy was in the terrible two's and smart as a whip! I did have a hard time handling him. I did not believe in spanking or hitting. I just tried to reason with a two year old. He was sweet and wanted to do

16

whatever I asked. I didn't know consistent discipline and constructive consistency. I was haphazard.

It seems strange now as I write all this, that I was so young and careless. While I did go to church once in a while, and did study the bible, I was not stable. I was happy and thankful to be free and alive! But I smoked like a chimney! At least a pack a day! I drank and dated on the weekends.

I decided to move in to a small house with my sister and her little girl. A big yard and quite roomy. After some months she planned to get married and moved out. I let a young Dutch girl, that had lived in the same apartment building, move in with me in the little house. It was great and very comfortable. One morning we got up to a huge breakfast made in the middle of the kitchen floor! It was a dozen eggs cracked and mixed together with a box of flour! There sat Jimmy in the middle of the pile. He looked up at us with a smile and said, "Make pancakes Mommy!"

By this time, all was calm with my ex husband. He would visit once in a while and play with Jimmy. I was happy about that and encouraged it. It was only occasional, but at least he visited.

One night my room mate awoke, startled and frozen in fear. We were in the same room. Single, twin beds on each side of the small bedroom, with a night stand between the two beds. Jimmy was in a crib in the other room. He was sound asleep. I was in a deep sleep.

She heard the steps of something coming into our room. Then she saw a dark, clothed figure rise up off the floor. It came up and over me and swayed side to side, over me. It swayed and swayed, side to side. Then she watched in horror as it moved out of our bedroom. She heard it's steps slide on the floor and the swish of the cloth on it as it slid out of the room.

She woke me up screaming! We ran to check on Jimmy. He was still asleep. She tried to settle down and explain to me what she saw and heard. But I knew what she was talking about!

Whatever it was, it had come for me when I was sixteen. A girlfriend, spending the weekend, was with me in bed. We were both awake, at my older sister's home. It was the most frightening thing either of us had ever experienced! We could hear it moving across the room toward us! It was dark in the room, but she knew it was after me! We could feel it as pure evil! We both started screaming and screaming. My sister and her husband came running! We explained what we heard and felt. Horrible! Just horrible! As a Catholic, I went to the local priest the next morning. But he was no help at all.

So, my roommate moved out and left me with the little house all by myself with

Jimmy. But it was too much money, so I moved back to the apartment building. And we would picnic at the pool with other tenants. I had my family close by. They were always a comfort and company for Jimmy and me. Although we didn't have much, we did have a little black and white TV. We would share a small chicken pot pie sometimes for dinner. He would eat first and I would eat the crust. To this day, I am affected when I see those chicken pot pies!! Jimmy was bright, funny and a joy!

I was working part time and bought a used 1955 Chevy Bel Air. It was green and white and a wonderful car. I could get around to jobs and shopping. Jimmy would stand next to me or sit next to me with his juice. Those were happy times. No seat belts in those days. But I was always a good driver. There was a little play yard with gravel. His favorite thing was bath time with all his little plastic army men lined up on the edge of the tub. Put bubbles around them and knock them off.

A secretarial course was offered to women that were on any government program. AFDC, Aid to Families with Dependent Children was the main thrust of the college course. I qualified and was excited about getting back into the work place, but with a higher paying job. It was a full day and held on a college campus near by. About twenty young women. We used the college class rooms as we were scheduled when they were not in use. A six hour a day and four days a week. Everything for an office was covered! It was intense cramming! A few of us girls commuted together. Jimmy was just across the street in a small family day care and with a grandma type lady. Sweet lady, that loved Jimmy.

I began to date Morris again, the person that I met after my divorce. I had settled down more and didn't feel so resentful about his attentiveness. We talked about getting married after I was through with the secretarial course in May. That was only around three months away! I was thrilled and tried to plan where we would live? But Morris felt he needed more money! A nest egg! So he informed me that he needed to return to Alaska and to a short job there that would pay him a lot of money. We could get married when he returned. I begged and pleaded with him not to go. The money was not worth it. We could work it out, together.

He wanted me to drive him to the airport. I did. I told him our lives would be forever changed. If he left, our destiny would not be the same. It would be altered. I knew it. But he got on the plane and was gone.

I went back to classes and continued on with school. I wrote to Morris and did not get a response. Nothing. No letters. I wrote more often and watched the mail — nothing. Weeks went by and no response. Then a month with no letter! I began to not feel well. Within weeks, I found I was pregnant. I wrote to Morris that I was pregnant, but that it was OK. I was happy to be. I would wait for him.

Finally a letter came! But it was a scathing, horrible letter! An awful and hateful letter. I cried and cried and didn't know what to do. I finished the class and got a good grade. It had a secretarial certificate of completion from the college. But it meant nothing now as I realized I was in big trouble. I contacted a social worker and we laid out a plan that I could have medical and deliver the baby at a county hospital. If I chose to not keep the baby, then I would have the option at that time. It seemed I had no choice as I got bigger and bigger and the months went by. My girlfriend and her family would watch Jimmy while I was away.

I met Michael to have lunch and catch up, he had gotten married! I had a raincoat on and was seated in the booth when he arrived. I didn't get up. He never knew I was pregnant. It would be many years before we would see each other again.

I entered the hospital a few weeks before my delivery. There were no doctors on the evening at the time of the delivery. The nurse frantically called for help. But I was left alone and delivered the baby by myself. A beautiful and perfect baby boy. The nurse came back and was so upset! As though I could have not delivered the baby! I yelled back at her that I couldn't help it! She cut the cord and took the baby with her and called for the doctor again.

I stayed another week at the hospital and saw the baby each day as I made my plan.

My family picked me up and brought me home to my sister's apartment. She was now divorced with her son, five years old. Jimmy was there and I kneeled down to take him in my arms. But he said "I don't know you".

I said gently to him, "It's Mommy!"

He said, "No. My Mommy died. You look like my Mommy, but my Mommy died!"

I hugged him and hugged him and assured him that it was me! He slowly came around to being affectionate, but I was worried. Deep inside I felt that the separation from him might have been too traumatic. But he seemed to be happy and well as time went by.

I decided that I did want to keep my baby. I called the social worker and told her so. My family was against it! The social worker said that I did not have adequate means to prove I could support the baby and that I would have to go to court now to prove my case and take custody. I did not have a place to live and would have to name the father and take him to court. I would not be eligible for any assistance if I did not sue the father. But now I didn't even know where he was located. I couldn't fight without any support. Jimmy and I had nothing, not even a place to live.

I gave up and let the baby be placed in adoption and signed the papers.

Mom and Dad came to visit my sister and me and play with the grandchildren. Mom was doing well as she was on medications. The hysterectomy that she underwent in the sanitarium had really made a huge difference in her well being. The medications from the 1959 time period were working well with her. I told them I needed a good job and perhaps I could find one near them. They wanted Jimmy and me to come and stay with them while I looked for work.

And so we moved in with them down the peninsula, south of San Francisco. A perfect area and I was away from any small town gossip. I did find the perfect job with a law firm. Mom was great with Jimmy and she loved watching him. It was a large apartment and had an enclosed play yard downstairs. Things were well and I settled into my new job.

Jimmy was around 4 1/2 now and a ball of fire! Mom said they were out playing and watering the flower bed. She let him water and he put the hose into the old lady's window down stairs! Everyone screamed and Jimmy dropped the hose! He was funny, quick and mischievous! A handful for Mom, but she loved being with him. I tried to watch her medication schedule. I would count to try to make sure she was not missing any doses. I began to notice bouts of severe agitation.

I confronted her and she was furious with me. Yelling at me that, "You are not my child, you belong to Wilma". That was my aunt. I talked to Dad about the growing agitation, when missing her medicine.

We were on the second story and the stairs were beginning to worry me. Jimmy had almost fallen down them. We did not have enough bedrooms and were cramped. I was beginning to worry about the long hours that Mom was watching Jimmy. So I discussed, with only Dad, that I was going to look for a larger place to live.

After searching and interviewing prospects, I decided to move in with a young woman and her two children. A beautiful large home in Atherton. Her husband had recently died in a terrible car accident. She welcomed the company and I agreed to have her watch Jimmy during the day. We moved in and everyone had their own large bedrooms! The next door neighbors had a pool and we spent the summer swimming! Jimmy was in swim classes at the local rec center. He loved the water and learned quickly.

We were happy there. Christmas came and it was a fun time with her extended family. Jimmy and I went to our family too. All was well.

I decided to put Jimmy in Nursery School, two days a week. That way he would be getting ready for kindergarten. Just a short drive down the country road and close to home. He did very well and seemed to enjoy the time spent with others.

Easter came and went and it was a lot of fun with the two other children. We lived in a very luxurious home. Professionally decorated and hardwood floors through out. We always came in through the laundry room, which was tiled. That entrance was in the driveway, just past the kitchen. So not too far from the front entrance hall doors. I was at work and Joyce was watching Jimmy that day. When I came home that evening, she asked me to sit down and talk with her. She said that they came in the back door, as they always did, and she started to take his shoes off. He was turning five shortly. She said something happened to him. He did not look like himself and was distraught and uncontrollable.

I said "No, he couldn't have!"

She said that I needed to seek help. No! He is easy to watch. He couldn't have done anything like that.

It began a breakdown in our friendship. I just could not believe her. I made my plan to move out.

I do remember driving to work one morning, late. Had to get Jimmy to a new Nursery School! Had to find a new place to live! I was getting scared! I remember being frantic! Too much pressure! I turned and yelled at him, "You have to be good!! We will be in trouble if you don't be good!"

I remember the terrified look on his face as I yelled!

I found a small apartment within driving distance to work. It had a pool and I felt that being alone with Jimmy, would ease any pressure from others. The weather was turning warm and we could swim every day. I found a large preschool near work. I would drop him off on my way each morning.

We made a lot of friends at the apartment complex. There was a park next door and we would walk there after work, to play on the equipment.

One evening at bedtime, we were saying our prayers. "Our Father, which art in heaven…".

All of a sudden, Jimmy jumped out of bed and threw himself against the wall! He curled up in a ball and started screaming, "Don't hurt me. Don't hurt me". He was in a terror. Utter terror!

I leaped to him and pulled him into my arms! Calling to him. It's Mommy! It's Mommy! Don't be frightened!

He was screaming and arms swinging! Then he went limp in my arms and looked into my eyes and said, "Mommy, what's happening to me?"

21

Then he switched and became extremely distraught.

This lasted for about a half hour. I was so frightened! I held him and he was exhausted and fell asleep.

Perhaps the stress of it all was getting to him too! My stress. Not enough money to get by. Always hurrying to work and back. My brother-in-laws had always fought with me, saying that I was not a good mother. Maybe they are right?

But all was well for a few weeks. Then one evening, driving home from work, Jimmy tried to jump out of the moving car! I pulled over and got control of him. He said he wanted to hurt himself.

The next morning I made an appointment to take him in to Stanford.

After the preliminary meeting with Pediatrics, Jimmy was observed behind a one way mirror. The doctor and I sat quietly, together, while his assistant worked and played with Jimmy for over an hour.

His conclusion was that Jimmy was very bright and well advanced for his age. Well coordinated and socially skilled and friendly. Nothing wrong at all, that he could see! Well adjusted. I thanked him and we left.

But as we left the building, Jimmy switched! I had to hang on to him in the parking lot. He was angry and furious! Ranting and furious. I didn't know what to do. Eventually he became exhausted and tired and I got control. Things calmed down and we went home.

So I moved again. Closer to work! Four blocks away. I could get to him quickly, if necessary. But all was well at the nursery school. A large school and the elderly woman who ran it, was especially fond of Jimmy! So all seemed to calm down again. But I felt a certain doom? I was frightened and couldn't shake it.

It was time to enroll Jimmy in public school. He was certainly well ahead of his age level. I was very confident that he would handle it just fine.

It was a half a day and then the remainder spent at the nursery school. It was so close to work that it went very smoothly.

But within three days, I received a telegram from the Santa Clara Co. Probation Dept. They wanted me to get in Touch with them. Now I knew where my fear was centered.

I was frightened, but I called them. I had to go in for an interview. They said I had been reported as being unable to control and guide my son. I suspected it was the kindergarten teacher! But they would not tell me who had turned me in. They said they believed I needed help. Perhaps medical help with Jimmy? They said if I allowed partial physical custody they would do a full medical work up. Otherwise they would take me to court and take custody! They said if I cooperated, he would get the best of medical attention. I was afraid of them! But I agreed with the plan.

A worker came to the nursery school and took him for a medical work up. But it did not go as I planned and they were going to try to keep him from me! I talked to my boss, an Attorney, and he said we should go into court! I did and told the court it was a medical problem! I needed to get him medical attention, not lose custody! The court agreed and I took him to a neurologist. A leading specialist, highly recommended.

He did a series of interviews and tests. It was shown that Jimmy was having petite mall seizures! He showed me as he was having them! It was only in his eyes that it was seen. The doctor said that we must get him on medication to stop them and he needed to be in a very controlled setting to test different medications. The first medications made it worse and more violent. I did visit Jimmy as they were testing him. It was awful! He was angry at me and just hated me for what I was doing! Dr. Van Meter, the neurologist, tried another medication. He needed him on it for a few days to test the results.

But as Jimmy was getting worse, I was slipping! I was driving to see him at the confined setting where they were medicating him. As I was driving, my body started to contract. All my muscles started to feel like they were shrinking! My chest muscles were collapsing! I couldn't breathe. I pulled over to the side of the freeway and stopped the car. My face felt as though it was shriveling and shrinking! My hands and fingers were curling inward! It was horrifying! A man came up to the window and told me to just sit! That I was having some kind of a reaction! I didn't move. And slowly my body began to return to normal. I was horrified at what had happened to me. I told Jimmy's neurologist about it and he prescribed medication for me. He felt it might be anxiety attack and fear or something? Perhaps he would give me medicine to slow my heart rate? That would stop the attack. The next day, after work, co-workers and I stopped on our way home for salads. There was a Halloween party going on in the bar and restaurant. It was loud and horrible and ugly. Their costumes were gruesome! I walked out and went home.

I was getting ready for bed and I looked in the mirror. As I brushed my teeth, I looked into my own eyes and felt sorry. Sorry that my life had turned out like it had. I was only twenty six years old, but I knew I was finished. I was making Jimmy worse and could not help him. The doctors were telling me that I was causing his problems. I believe them now. I was causing his seizures? And now to have this new problem of attacks that are crippling? I looked again in the mirror into the dark face and I felt tired. Too tired to go on. This life was not as I would have expected! I can not face another day of the horror of it. It is too ugly. I can't even help my son. "I am sorry" I said to the person looking back at me in the mirror. Perhaps someone will be able to help Jimmy. I feel helpless again and weak.

So I got the bottle of pills. The pills that the neurologist had made me promise, I would not abuse. I carefully took the whole bottle. And then I took a bottle of aspirin. I laid down in bed and covered myself. I drifted away. I was roused a little and saw a circle with a bright light behind it. I thought that it was an angel and I had gone to heaven.

I awoke a few days later in the hospital. The angel turned out to be a policeman's rounded helmet with glaring light behind him. There were no angels. And I was not in heaven! I was in pain! Tubes were in my throat. I drifted in and out of consciousness for the next day. Then I was placed in a psychiatric ward in a hospital bed! I was in a County General Hospital.

I woke up slowly. There were two other women in the room. They were very quiet and still. I was weak and could hardly move. The large door to the main hall opened and a very fat man came into the room. He sat down on the side of my bed. He was so fat! The perspiration was dripping off his forehead. Some was moving down the side of his cheeks. There was a cigar in his mouth and a bit of drool was coming out one side of his mouth and dripping down. I could smell his sweat and the stink of the cigar! He patted my knee and leaned closer to me.

He smiled at me and said, "Now Dearie, you really didn't mean to hurt yourself, did you?"

I didn't move. I just looked at him. He was unkempt! His shirt, that should have been white, was dirty and wrinkled.

He said, "I am your psychiatrist. You will be here for a week. You will participate in group therapy each day. You will be evaluated and then, hopefully, released in a week.

He smiled and looked at me. His mouth was still slobbery. I thought to myself, if this seated before me, that is absurd, represents sanity, then I have gone mad.

My son's neurologist came to visit me. He was so angry that he had trusted me with the medications for my heart. He told me he was now my doctor, too. He would take charge of everything. He told me I was still insured at work. He was going to send me away to a facility that would care for me. There would be psychiatric group therapy that I could participate in. He and his wife would come and supervise my care.

I couldn't speak. He left.

My best girlfriend got through on the pay phone in the lounge. A patient got it and handed me the phone.

My friend said, "It's alright, perhaps no one understands your pain. And if they did, they would have let you die".

She hung up. I couldn't speak anyway. But something clicked in my head! It was so honest! It was like the first real true statement I had heard in a long time! I never forgot it and I never forgot her! She has been a forever friend! While the words were brutal, a strange awareness had clicked somewhere deep inside me. It was far away. Somewhere far removed from me.

In group each day, I found the people very intelligent and interesting. Most were married and working. Some alcoholics had tried to take their lives. Everyone had tried to hurt themselves. But they all seemed so normal! I liked them all. I still couldn't speak. But I smiled sometimes, at them as they finished speaking. We all sat in a huge circle. It was supervised with a doctor and nurse. No one pushed me to try to speak.

Then the week was over. My aunt came into the ward to take me to my apartment. I was being released to her. While signing out on the floor, I became reluctant. I did not want to go through the big doors to go out to the outer hallway! I started to cry. I opened my mouth, to the nurse, to try and tell her! But no sound would come out. It was as though my brain was not wired to my mouth! I made hand gestures to the nurse about the big doors! I kept pointing to my throat and my mouth!

She put her hand on my shoulder and said,

"It is very common, that when people shut down, then they are in a safe place, and don't want to leave".

She said, "You must leave!"

I went out in the hall. My aunt was waiting there. She walked me to her car and asked, "Which way is your apartment?"

I had lived there four years, and now I couldn't remember which way to go! I seemed to be disoriented as far as north and south, east and west? Finally she found where I lived and dropped me off. I packed my station wagon of everything I owned and drove away.

I drove to the Santa Cruz mountain area. High up a country, wooded road, I found Bridge Mountain Facility. It was on the top of the mountain forest, overlooking the valley below. They knew I was arriving and I signed all the necessary papers. There was a staff of about fifteen. They told me they received guests on the weekends that participated in group encounters and classes from leading therapists and doctors. I was not expected to do anything. I was not expected to talk. There were no expectations for me at all. My doctors would visit soon and advise them how I was doing. They showed me to a small room that I would share with a young woman my age. She was a staff member . I was alone and I unpacked.

25

It was quiet and I did not speak to anyone. I walked around during the day and looked everything over. There was a music building, with a piano. I began to play the piano again. My brain seemed to begin to work when I played piano. No guests were there during the week and so I was alone. In a large library, I found a book on "Natural Meditation". Just being quiet and still. Going within. I began to read the bible and other spiritual books. I was allowed to use the large art building, where group art therapies were held on the weekends. I began to paint again. I was getting stronger and stronger. So I began to wash dishes in the kitchen. No one spoke to me, as they thought I was crazy and I am sure they were afraid of me.

But eventually, I spoke. It was while we were clearing the dishes. A few weeks had passed and they felt I was a hard worker and they were thanking me. It opened the door to more speaking. But I noticed that I could not speak the truth. It was as though there was a disconnect between my brain and my tongue! If someone asked me a question, I would answer, with a slightly off, reply.

"How many hours had I been in the kitchen?" If it was an hour, I would answer 45 minutes. If I woke up at 6 am, I would say 7 am. It frightened me because I was working at getting better. I wanted to do everything I could to get better and have my son back. I had to get well. So I devised my own method. I would talk slower, if I had to speak. If I did not tell the truth, on the smallest matter, I would go back. Tell the person that I did not tell the correct answer, or that I just told an untruth, and now, tell it exactly right.

It worked! I began to make the connection in my brain and speak clearly and truthfully. But I had to speak very, very slowly. I did talk to a visiting therapist about the truth and speaking the truth. He explained that it was a defense mechanism. I could present a false self. An imposter, because the truth would allow someone to be close to me. Even though it was embarrassing, I had to repeat myself all the time.

I enjoyed working with everyone, even though it wasn't necessary. The staff was kind and helpful. Eventually I was invited to join some of the weekend therapy groups. I stayed on the sidelines most of the time. But if it was a very gentle and soft, group encounter, I would try to join in. I learned a lot and tried to be more open. I met a lot of the leaders of the groups and the doctors. I met Kriyananda, a student of Paramhansa Yogananda. This is a quote of his thoughts on "Bridge Mountain":

"In search of clarity of another kind, I used also to travel south to Ben Lomond, near Santa Cruz, California, where a group called Bridge Mountain held programs that were slanted differently from what I was accustomed to. They involved students rather than only lecturing to them. I was intrigued, and wanted to draw from what they did any benefits I could, for my own teaching.

"Thus, another world opened to me: the self-help or "self-actualization" movement.

Students in the classes would make surrealistic drawings supposed to express their inner fears, anxieties, and motivations. I had no fears that I was aware of, but the leaders claimed that everyone harbors such psychological complexes.

"I remember telling a member of the staff, Pat Kutzner, who for a time was my secretary, after Bridge Mountain closed-that I'd never known my parents to have a falling out. "That can only mean," she replied dismissively, "that one of them is suppressing a lot of frustration!" Well, I'd seen no evidence that this was so. Nor had anyone I'd ever known. My father's droll explanation for the harmony between them was to say, "When my wife and I were first married, I told her I would make all the important decisions in our marriage. Since then," he concluded with a grin, "there haven't been any important decisions to make!" None so important, anyway, as to come between them.

"I went along with what was taught at Bridge Mountain, however, because it seemed a good place to learn an aspect of what was in vogue those days.

"That was also the time of "Primal Scream" therapy, and other methods of venting suppressed frustrations: "letting it all hang out," as the expression was, that people might regain the uncomplicated freedom of their primordial nature. Those were also the days when people met for "honest confrontation." They'd pair off, face each other, and announce "honestly" just what bothered them about one another. It was all meant to relieve them of inner tensions. What it really did, of course, was induce tension. I never saw people purged of animosity by these treatments.

"At Bridge Mountain we threw wads of mud at a board to vent our anger, thereby, supposedly, releasing it from the subconscious. I tried to join in the fun, though in fact I couldn't think of anything to vent, not even anger against Self Realization Fellowship, in Berkeley. It seemed to me this approach was all wrong. I wanted, however, to learn what people were thinking and doing to improve themselves. The leaders at Bridge Mountain made kindly excuses for me. No doubt, they seemed to feel, I'd dig up something from my subconscious eventually, and discover the boiling cauldron I'd been suppressing. For my part, I thought I might learn a few ideas for conducting classes involving students instead of only lecturing to them. Eventually, I realized that in fact I was involving them already, in a subtler way. What I did, and still do, was tune in to them spiritually, and commune in my spirit with their spirits. People have often come to me after a lecture and thanked me for clarifying a problem they've been having. I've never discouraged others, however, from seeking ways to involve students in the learning process. Basically, Bridge Mountain's idea in doing so seemed good to me, even though I still consider the emphasis on releasing the subconscious a mistake, generally speaking. All it does, according to my observation, is affirm one's own negative tendencies."
     end of quote...............

As I became stronger and stronger physically, my mind was healing. Nothing was going to stop me now from complete wholeness! I knew going within and looking and searching was the right path.

My doctor and his wife came to visit and were pleased that I was doing so well. They set up a visit for me with my son.

My son was not that far away. When I was in the hospital, Dr. Van Meter placed him in a residential treatment center, that had an elementary school. He was within 45 minutes of the therapy center I was living in.

Visits with my son were heartbreaking. He didn't understand why he was not with me. I didn't understand it at all, either? I just knew I made him angry and they said that tension caused the petite mall seizures.

He was a healthy, big boy! Just emotionally charged and in pain from being separate from me. Inside myself I vowed to keep getting better.

Chapter Three

A Group Encounter at Bridge Mountain

As I was growing and becoming more active in work, in the kitchen, and help cleaning, sweeping the walkways, the staff trusted me more. I was open about not telling any untruths. It was intense interaction with the staff and therapists. Sometimes very painful and embarrassing. It was always meant to expose and get under the surface of your cover. I could feel that there was something wrong with me. I couldn't reach it though. It was only a deep, intuitive haunting ache, that wouldn't go away. But my eyes were beginning to open to the world inside.

I was asked to join in the encounter group, on a special weekend. The group consisted of about 30 people and a lot of the staff was joining in. It was a game, like musical chairs! The men in the inner circle and the women in the outer circle. The music played a simple childish tune, that you sang to the man in front of you, as you looked at his face. Just four minutes and the music would stop. The men moved to the right one place when the music stopped. You were not to speak at all, just sing the song as the music played. I thought it was a little stupid and childish. Just silly, but I did it. About 20 minutes in, the music stopped for everyone to scoot to the next person. We were in the huge auditorium with beautiful hardwood floors to scoot onto the next pillow.

The music stopped. Two staff members in front of me got mixed up. They bumped into each other! One went to the left. So it meant that two were coming toward me! They thought it was funny! I must have looked frightened! So they crawled closer to me!

I put my hands up and started yelling at them, "Wait a minute! Wait a minute! Wait a minute" Then something was happening to my brain. I heard an echo of "Wait a minute!" It was far away.

So I screamed at them! "Wait a minute"!

Everything went black. I was falling into blackness. But I could hear a little girl screaming, far, far away. But as I was falling, the faint voice was getting louder and louder! She was screaming "wait a minute, wait a minute!" I could tell she was getting closer and closer as she was louder and more piercing! I recognized the voice. The sound was me and I fell into the scream and we became one. I was the scream. I fell into myself.

I opened my eyes and was back! I was conscious and horrified that I remembered the rape when I was 12 years old. I jumped up and started crying and running in circles! Then I ran out the door and was going to run away, down the road! Run, run, I thought! Run!

But one of the guys, the staff member, was chasing me! He was yelling and screaming at me, but he couldn't catch me!

Then he yelled, "Go ahead and run, you fool! There is no place to run to get away from yourself! There is no place to go!"

I heard him. I heard the truth. I stopped. I turned around, broken inside, and walked slowly back to Bridge Mountain. No one spoke to me. I spoke to no one for a few days. No one ever asked me what happened. I was getting better. I remembered that I begged to not be raped. I remembered that I kept saying "Wait a minute! Wait a minute". The two boys came at me and it was similar during the encounter group.

I had a bit, of my little girl self, back. Back to grow and be well and OK. But it was very slow going. I had a new sense of awareness, that I had been functioning, with something so huge, going on deep inside me. I had always remembered the incident when I was so young, but I seemed to feel nothing about it, until I heard the scream. I always knew that my childhood had been horrific, but I thought I was OK, because I didn't feel anything. I thought I was strong and brave for just surviving! I was alive!

Chapter Four

Vision of a Supernatural Revealing

I was different. It was as though I was bigger and growing together inside. When I looked at something, I was really seeing as though I had been unaware before. Looking as though I was seeing and experiencing for the first time.

I stepped up my visits with my son on the weekends. We would stay in a close by motel and I tried to make sure they had a good pool. He was a good swimmer and loved the water.

I was painting again. The best I had ever done. I knew I was really in Touch with my inner self. I was learning everything I could, every chance I could.

Then one night, about 4 am, I was awakened. I was laying flat on my back as I awoke. Above me, about two to three feet above me, was a huge skull, very white with darkness behind and all around it! I guess it was about two feet in circumference! I thought I was asleep and I rubbed my eyes and open and closed my eyes! But it was still just above me. Suddenly the skull faded away, by the replacement of a beautiful white and glowing lamb. Just the head area and a bit of its neck. It was glowing and beautiful! Glowing white and a slight golden glow. Then the skull, death, was there again! Huge! Then the Lamb was there and it replaced death. It transposed perhaps three to four times! I fainted.

When I awoke the next morning, I didn't know what to make of it? I knew it meant something, symbolically, but didn't know what? But I would keep it to myself. I told no one.

I made some close friends. This was the sixties and most people smoked marijuana or took drugs and got high. I was terrified of anything that would affect my mind. I was trying so hard to take care of my mind. So everyone was very careful around me. People came from all over to visit Bridge Mountain, as it was somewhat famous. The staff had become family to me and they all knew how hard I was trying to get well.

Some of the visitors to Bridge Mountain came from a commune a few miles away. It was called the "North Star". It was owned by the Livingstons. It was a large old hunting lodge from the 20's or 30's. There were other communes in the valley, but some of them were just too strange for me to visit. And some communes were very dangerous. Sometimes there were just too many drugs and the whole experience went downhill. People got hurt and some died. I was seeing what the damaging affects of many, hard drugs could do. I did not see any good come out of any drug use. But everyone tolerated me and I was allowed to move freely among anyone and anyplace. They considered me safe. Many people went mad. But for me, I knew that I was growing and learning at a lightning speed! Living with 25 to 30 people at a time was raw, group therapy! It was brutal, but I knew I was getting better. Going within to see what was wrong with me was the answer.

One evening I was at a friend's house, just being quiet and away from so many people at Bridge Mountain. I was really deep in thought. Still trying to search inside myself for what was wrong. Examining and searching and looking. I reflected on my life as far back as I could remember, back to a child. I reflected on everything I had done. I considered everything I could remember. I turned my thoughts back upon past experiences. Suddenly, I was really taking a good honest look! It was as though all the buried memories were looked upon for the first time! I felt shame at what I saw! I saw always excusing any wrong doing, by me, by just moving on. Moving on quickly, so I wouldn't feel anything! Like remorse! Or guilt! Wrong decisions I had made. Horrible choices. I couldn't shake it and now there was no way to block really looking at myself! It was as though I had opened my heart to look at what was wrong? I couldn't shut the door now. Things my mind had buried, were now exposed and I couldn't hide from myself. Wrong choices again and again! I didn't want to look or remember anymore!

"Is there nothing good in me? Am I all bad?" I said to myself.

To myself, in my defense, I cried out, "I love my son!" This part of my life must be good!

I was trying to grasp at something good in me!

I was removed from me. I was separate! I couldn't feel. It was as though it wasn't me? I was separate from the things I had done! I was separated from myself that I had created. And that self I was looking at was really me! But I was disconnected from her!

I was split! My spirit! Oh my God, that's me! All of that, that I really looked at, is me! All that I have done separate from my soul or spirit is really me. There I was! I was shocked at myself! I faced it and accepted my past. And I accepted myself, as bad as I was, I was me!!! I pulled this broken, bad, pitiful, sinner, awful girl, to myself. This is who I am! This is ME! Oh my God, it's me!!!!

I will never be able to describe the completeness and joy that I felt for the first time in my life! I was one and I could feel. I was so excited and happy! I was one person!! I didn't want to lose it. How can I keep this? In order to live a life and feel, I've got to remember all this! How can I remember all that I learned about my wrong choices, so I won't separate again? I don't want to hurt myself again. Doing whatever I consider wrong, will hurt me and I will separate again!

Well, it's no to what is wrong!! I will make my choices from this new, complete self. And yes, to what is right. So, if there is a yes and a no? Is there a wrong and a right? There has got to be a good and a bad! I was desperate to hold myself together and trying hard to understand. Good and bad! I felt very aware of a knowledge of good and evil! Good and evil! I felt very excited. I concluded that there was a good and evil! Then God is good. Yes, then there really is a God! And I knew it in my whole being. This put together person, all of a sudden, knew there was a God. I could feel it! I was right! It was as though I always knew! For eternity! Everything was true. It was all true about God. And goodness. And the joy of it all, was knowing. It was as though I remembered! I remembered it all, deep in my soul and spirit! As though I had been gone for a long time. I had been far away from myself. God is good!

Well, if there is a God and I can remember it, and feel this joy, then He must have had a son, too! That's true too, then!! There must be a Son of God, Jesus Christ. I concluded it. I had figured it out! I knew the truth and I wanted to go and tell my friend! I was elated and I raised my lowered head, up from my hands. I needed to go and look for him and tell him all I had just figured out!

I can only attempt to tell, in my stumbling way, what happened next. It's been almost a half century now, and I still cry, if I speak of it. If I hadn't been directed by God to write, I wouldn't write. And I wouldn't tell.

Across the room I saw my friend. But, superimposed, about an inch in front of him, magnified in front of him, I saw the Christ Jesus. The Holy Spirit was magnifying through, in front of my friend! I started screaming and screaming!

"Oh my God! Oh my God!" I just kept screaming and screaming!

I couldn't bear to look! I was crying and crying!

My friend grabbed me by the shoulders and was holding on to me. He yelled,

"What's wrong with you"?

I looked again, into the face! I could see Him!

Into my heart, silently, gently, He spoke, "He can't see me and he doesn't understand."

I tried to be quiet and gain control of myself. I was afraid to look! I tried to hide my face. I couldn't stop crying.

But then I lifted my face, to look.

He looked at me! In the look from Him, I remembered that He had been crucified! Agony! I flew backwards and to the floor with an impact! I remembered Him. And that I loved Him! It was agony! I cried and cried!

My friend was seated in front of me, frozen! I got up, partially, to my knees. I was within an arms length to Him. I wanted to look again! So I did. I could still see Him, magnified, just in front of my friend! I could see Him still!!

In my heart I cried out, "Why, why did you take so long? Why did you take so long?"
I blamed Him!

Still magnified and just inches in front of my friend, He reached out and put His hand on my forehead. I saw just whispers of lives go by. Like a breeze was lightly, flipping pages of a book. It was like a mist moving by, with a lifetime in it. Gentle. I don't know? Perhaps 10 or a 100 or a 1000 lifetimes? I don't know? It didn't make any difference. I just said in my heart, to myself, "Oh yes, Oh yes". It was me that took so long. I missed the mark. There was no one else there to blame. Not my parents. Not my brutal ex husband. No one but me. I missed the mark. It was always me. I understood. He was always waiting. He was always there. I became aware that time was standing still. It wasn't passing.

Then, with His hand still in my forehead, I went out into outer darkness, into the universe. My soul was separate from God. Separation because of all that I was and had done. I was alone and I existed. It was the same place, as when I died in surgery, years before. It was hell in eternity! No words can describe my terror!

I returned in an instant and would surely have gone mad!

But He silently spoke into my heart and soul, and said:

"IT'S ALRIGHT BECAUSE OF ME YOU ARE SAVED. YOU BELONG TO ME."

34

I cried, from sheer joy, "Oh my God! Oh my God!" I was so thankful and happy! I was saved from the separation! I felt such love for Him! Not of this world. It can not be lived in this world. Not in this life experience.

Then He said: "IT IS OVER. YOU MUST LEAVE."

"But where will I go and what will I do?" I asked.

Everything was spoken to me in a silent voice that went straight into my heart. It was very powerful and went into my soul and memory.

It was over.

I told my friend, who was speechless and eyes huge, that we must leave. I reached for my pack of cigarettes. I had smoked since I was fourteen. My arm was stopped short of grasping them!

The Lord's big voice said:

"YOU WILL NEVER NEED THOSE AGAIN!"

I drew my hand back as if I touched a hot iron! Almost a half a century has passed now and I never smoked again. The desire was gone. The addiction was healed.

Silently, we went outside and got in the car.

I called out to Him, with the silent voice of my heart, "Don't leave me! Please don't leave me!" I begged. I pleaded. I yelled as loud as I could with the voice of my heart!

I looked again, toward my friend, in the passenger side of the front seat of the car. I could still see the Lord magnified.

Then He silently said:

"I WILL NEVER LEAVE YOU OR FORSAKE YOU, I WILL BE WITH YOU FOREVER".

"But I won't be able to see you! I want to be able to see you! I have to see you! Don't leave me!" I demanded.

He said: "YOU WILL SEE ME IN THE FACE OF EVERYONE WHO COMES THROUGH THE DOOR."

That was it. With all His authority, His words went straight into my heart and soul, forever! I did not question the statement, even though I did not understand. The sound of His voice went into my heart and my mind, unquestionably!

I was at peace.

We drove back to Bridge Mountain as though nothing had happened. My world had changed forever. I was a put together person for the first time in my life. I went to bed and the presence of the Lord was with me. It was restful and perfect. Happiness that would be mine, only for a time. As I started to fall asleep, into my heart, silently, the words were spoken:

"YOU MUST LEAVE HERE AND GO TO THE NORTH STAR HOUSE. YOU ARE A SERVANT OF CHRIST. THERE WILL BE A GATHERING."

I drifted off into a deep sleep.

Chapter Five

Moving to the North Star Commune

(I asked some questions of the Lord, on January 24, 2012, almost fifty years after this experience. The "Touch" revealed:

"THIS WAS A DEEP SPIRITUAL EXPERIENCE.")

So the next morning I informed the staff that I was moving. I told them I was meant to go to the large commune, "North Star House". Of course they thought it was a terrible mistake! A terrible choice of a place to live! But I packed my clothes and few belongings and loaded my station wagon and left.

It wasn't that far, just a few miles away. I parked and climbed up the massive front stairs. It was a huge imposing hunting lodge. Three stories tall, of redwood. With dark wood stairs onto a massive porch. The front door was massive with a few small glass windows in the top center. I knocked loudly. I knew there were 25 to 35 people living on the property. There were seven private cabins with bathroom sinks and some with full bathrooms. The owners of the property lived a little way up a trail, in a nice home.

They heard my knocking at the main front door and let me in. I informed them that I was moving in. I said, "I was sent there by God".

They got the leaders and head of the house and brought them to me. It was a husband and wife.

They asked, "What are you trying to do? Take over and control this place?"

I said, "No. If anyone tries to take over or be leader of anyone, they will be gone! No one should control another."

I stood my ground and told them, "I was going, now, to visit the owners of the property and inform them also. I had no fear! What could I fear if God had told me to come here? It wasn't my idea! I was just excited about what might happen next! I figured that Jesus was right there with me, since He told me to come here.

So I was very, very happy to see each one of them. To look into their eyes and figure that each one was special to God, somehow! It absolutely didn't matter in the least, that they didn't like me! I loved them! Each one as I met them, I loved them all the same! If I came close to them or looked at them, I loved them. They didn't like it!

But they were helpless in front of me.

So I went down the short path to the owners and told them I was meant to be there. To my surprise, they agreed! They said the property was to be used as a meditation center. To the betterment and enrichment of each person that was allowed to be there. They felt that there was drug use and that it should be stopped. I told them I did not know why I was sent there, except that I was a "servant". That was all.

"I didn't like drugs, but that was not my business," I told them.

I moved in with a mixture of all kinds of different feelings towards me. My room was on the main floor. I went down a long hall, with walls of dark redwood. The bedrooms were large with high, high ceilings. It was so huge that your footsteps would echo as you walked through the halls and rooms! In the dining room there was a massive fireplace. It backed a fireplace in the living room. Eight huge bedrooms were on the main floor. A large bathroom was between every two of the bedrooms. Then a large separate tub and toilet, bathroom at the end of the hallway. A tiny, dark and curvy staircase led up to the next floor. On the next floor there was a great room with hardwood floors and a ceiling almost two or three stories up. Open raftered in redwood! It was spectacular. There were six bedrooms and baths on this second floor. This floor had a small library! It had a variety of books that became a treasure to me later.

It was clean and very nice and I settled in.

There was lots of work to do with that many people. Everyone needed to help. Some would try to take over and push others to perform tasks. Tensions could run high and there were lots of confrontations. Right away I was tagged as a goody two shoes. No one knew that I had just seen what a broken sinner I was. No one knew that I had just been put back together and saved by the Lord Himself! I told no one. So they tagged me as too good.

But there was wood to cut, stack and bring in when needed. The cooking of the evening meal was quite a task for so many mouths to feed. But it usually ran pretty smooth. There was always enough food to feed everyone. Many people that lived there had part time jobs. Jobs were plentiful. Some were artists and were selling in the local shops. But getting the PG&E paid every month was the biggest task! So it was a group effort and things did get done. I was so happy and joyous just to work! Anything and everything made me happy! I was a big irritant to most people. They did not want me to be that happy!

On the second day there, I was near the lower road, picking up chopped wood for the fire.

Three Jehovah's witnesses walked up the road and approached me. They began to tell me of God and Jesus and being saved.

I said, "I am saved! I know God! I have seen Jesus Christ magnified!"

Well they just looked at me like I was lying.

I said, "come close and look at my face. Can't you see me?"

"No. We can't see anything!"

"Come closer then and look into my eyes and see the truth!" I said!

"No. You didn't see Jesus Christ. We see nothing." They turned away and walked down the road.

I knew nothing could be seen in me. It didn't matter. I drove down the road to a pay phone and called my family and sister. I told them that "I knew God and had seen Jesus Christ magnified through a person. I had moved into a commune and I was saved. I was so happy!"

They all started crying! Sobbing. They said to come home "right now!"

"But I am where I am meant to be!" I said.

My sister cried and cried and told me that she was scared.

I learned immediately to keep my mouth shut. This was too big and too important to argue over or frighten people.

A few people from Bridge Mountain followed me to the commune, shortly after my move.

39

I knew I was well and healed. My insurance was ending and my workman's compensation was ending. I began to look for part time work, too. I brought my son to visit on the weekends, but we stayed in a motel just down the road. It had a pool and we could swim and visit my parents that lived close by. But it was very hard on my son to be separated from me. Very hard. Two of the counselors from the school where he was staying came to the commune. I was worried about the legal problems it might cause. Regarding visits. But they liked me and did not interfere with my visit schedule.

Chapter Six

The Experience of Going Into The Light

Tension in the commune escalated into, out and out fighting. Most people were guarded and defensive. Conflict within this close knit group was a pain! Underlying hate was so apparent that it would make the air thick! You could feel each others emotions. It was as though the cover was off each person. A lot of people had been exposed to group encounters. Some had experienced group therapy. So it was announced, by a majority of the residents, that we would have a group encounter to solve problems. It would be a 48 hour marathon. An encounter with no sleep or leaving the group! There were about 30 of us participating. Even though, some had been in groups, and some had even been leaders, this would be different for them. No one had been in sleep deprivation or a 48 hour marathon.

It got off to a good start and a lot of grievances were aired. But toward the second day, things really uncovered. There was such anger toward each other over small issues, that had never come to light. It was a fierce encounter. When they turned on me for loving them, I had no defense. It was as though I had been cleaned out inside. Only the love of God was in there now. It still came out toward them. I had to tell them the truth. I told them all that I had been healed and that it was God that put the love in there. I had been put back together by God. By the end of the encounter, so much was settled between enemies! Many of the old disputes dissipated. It was concluded that I must be a saint!

"But I was only a sinner", I told them. Me, who came from the depths of sin and hell, was not going to be their saint. They loved me now and it was agreed that they would protect me, in their way.

The leaders of the group, a husband and wife, had been in control for years. They moved out as the whole place was spiritually cleaned with the marathon. No one could be boss over another. And they couldn't function in that kind of freedom.

We were on the side of a hill that was in the Santa Cruz Mountains. It was situated at the end of a long isolated road. Sometimes neighbors would sit on their porches as we drove by. They sat with shotguns across their laps. We were hated by most of the tiny community at the beginning of that long road. I came from downtown Palo Alto, California. I had worked at a large Law Firm and my clothes were most appropriate. I looked straight, still. So I was sent down that long road to make peace with the neighbors. I looked normal and did not frighten them at all. They listened to me and guns were no longer displayed on that road.

I had a good car and did a lot of the needed driving and shopping. Some stores in the mountain area would not sell food or supplies to all of the people that I lived with. They were flower children. Beautiful long, long hair. Long clothes. Many dressed up in Renaissance style and some outrageous outfits! But always clean and beautiful. One very beautiful young woman, pregnant, could not rent a post office box. So I had to get it for her. I would go into any of the stores, because I looked and dressed straight. Merchants would sell to me, but not to my companions. I would intervene in the medical needs for them too. If they were really dressed up, sometimes in downtown Santa Cruz, people would spit at them. It was always a shock to me that these wonderful people, trying so hard to learn, could be so hated! So judged by most!

But I did not interfere with their lives. I would not preach to them. I Made a rule to myself. The rule was; if I was alone, with one person, and they asked why was I so happy? Only then, if asked, was I allowed to speak and explain. It worked and I seldom preached anything.

One day, after about a month, I went to the ocean with one of the men that lived in the North Star House. He was an older resident and had been there about a year. A quiet and sensitive man. His name was David. It was a beautiful summer day and very warm when we got to the coast. We climbed down a cliff and he went off to explore the rocks and walk down the beach. So I sat down, crossed legged, on the sand. The sand was hot and I took my shoes off and look out at the ocean. Just looking at the waves breaking and flowing toward me. The sun was causing a dazzling, sparkling, reflecting in my eyes! It was like a million dazzling diamonds. It was so beautiful. I was just thinking and reflecting on how blessed I was to have narrowly escaped death at my own hands. How glorious life was in this very moment! Just looking at the sparkling ocean. It was too beautiful. And this was always here, but I couldn't see it? Everything was waiting for me to see it! Waiting. I could remember. I could remember that we go back to remembering everything. We can go back to God. As I felt joy about knowing this, in an instant my vision or eyesight began to expand. As though I could see an area larger, around the sides of my view. It was blinding and warm. It was brighter than a million suns. In the lower part of my torso, below my belly button was a huge bolt or energy? I was frightened.

A big voice! Big! Inside my being, I think? Said:

"DO NOT FEAR   DO NOT BE FRIGHTENED."

The power moved to my center with a wave of light that was brighter! My stomach area was hit with a huge bolt of light and power energy!   Then the blinding light went to my chest area with power that I was barely able to take. Then it jumped to my right side chest area! It was all the pain I had ever known or endured in love or felt of love. Love of all I had known and loved and bore through good and bad pain. It was the love I had lived was felt as pain. I was dying. I couldn't stop it! I don't know if my heart was broken? Or it stopped? The wave of the blinding light and heat got bigger and stronger and jumped to my left side of my chest area and equal to the love I gave was an equal amount given to me of indescribable love from God to my entire self.

And then a blast of light greater, stronger than all the others, blasted through my heart area. I was made aware that God was searching my heart depths.

Did I want self worship?

No.

Another beam blasted through my heart! Greater than the last!

Did I love and worship God?

I Did

A greatest blast of light, the biggest passed through me. It was without words to tell.

I died. I remembered that I knew all the time. I knew all the time! (I will elaborate and explain this later in this book)

The light stopped. My face was burned! I went back to the commune. I told no one. The days following were spent in quiet peaceful thought about what had happened to me. Gradually the high spiritual state of mind left me. Everyone knew something big had happened to me, but they let me alone. I read more, studied and prayed and meditated. Searching, I found the light of God has been known of throughout time. Always known. We all know everything. We just get lost in the journey. It's the experience of life and searching everything out that leads us away from God and the light.

I began to mature more and more in my interaction with people. Living with, working with 25 to 30 people in close circumstances, will teach you fast. But I needed to leave. I needed a job. I was only working part time. My son needed me. I wanted to make a move and take my son back with me.

There was only one person that knew everything that I had experienced. He knew all. He was the head of a meditation center in San Francisco. He was a Christian. I called him. I told him that I wanted to leave. He said I was free to go. But it could be that I was needed right where I was.

I told him, "I don't do anything for them spiritually. I don't teach or tell them anything. No one knows what has happened to me, but you!"

He said, "It is in your presence that the balance hangs. In silence you teach. But you are free to go. You must have a great lesson to learn yet!"

He said, "Good-bye" and I never spoke to him again.

Chapter 7

Helping to Start a Meditation Center

I moved away and found full time work. I stepped up my visits with my son. I was back to just an everyday life and the daily tasks! But after months of trying to just work and visit my son on the weekends, I was wanting to move back. I rented a cottage near my son and Mom and Dad. I got in Touch with the owners of the property, of the commune. I arranged a visit with them. So we sat down and discussed what had taken place after I moved away. All hell broke loose! A very violent man had moved in when I left. He was mentally ill and had forced everyone out. The last two had just left. Two young women that he threatened and might have been physically violent with.

I told them that I still felt I should be there. They agreed. It was still meant to be a Christian prayer and meditation center. They asked me to come back.

So they told me I should go next door and inform the last person to leave. The dangerously ill man. Everyone had been afraid of him. The rumor, in the Valley, was that he had killed someone, that tried to stand up to him and get him to leave. But the property owners kept insisting that I was meant to be there.

I thought perhaps I would at least go into the building. Just to look around.

I thought no one was there. One of the main floor bedrooms must have had dogs living in it at one time. Dog and cat feces were all over the bedroom floor. The whole building was a disaster! Dirty and littered! I felt terrible. As if somehow responsible. I made my way through the halls and headed for the kitchen. It was a free swinging door into the kitchen. I pushed the door open and there he was!

I walked into the kitchen. I told him that I used to live there and that I knew the owners of the property.

He said, "Everyone is gone. And you should leave too!"

"But I am meant to be here." I said.

I told him, "I have just talked to the owners and they want me to come back to live here. I believe that you must go now."

It was within a split second that he had one arm around my shoulder and a huge knife was at my throat.

He said, "I'll kill you!"

To myself, I said, "Lord, I thought you wanted me to be here. I might die now."

I didn't move or flinch. I knew not to blink? I looked up into his eyes and held his gaze.

He looked into my eyes and said, "I will never leave here until I am loved!"

While still looking into his eyes I said, "I love you in the Lord Jesus Christ".

He put the knife down and without looking at me, he walked out the door and down the long road, away. He never came back.

I walked over to the owners and told them he was gone. We would start a meditation and prayer center now.

A lot of people from Bridge Mountain knew that we were looking for someone who was experienced in leading such an effort. There was an ad in the San Jose Mercury News of a person looking for a large building. To hold classes and lead a group. I called the local number and made arrangements to meet him.

I would interview him and get back to the owners with my decision.

So the plan was made to meet, this leader, in a very swank dinner house in downtown Los Gatos, California.

I arrived and found him right away. Sitting in the middle of the dining room was a yogi!

He had a full long beard and white clothes! I thought, "Oh no!"

So I sat down and ordered a salad. I began my long, long interview. To see if I could tell if this was the person I wanted to take with me, to build a Center!

He was Greek. His family had all come from Egypt. He was a Greek orthodox Christian.

Just married and lived next to his mother in San Jose. He told me where he went to college and every place he had ever lived. How he traveled around the world to find teachers. He would smile and look at me. He just kept answering my questions.

I don't know how long I questioned him. I just kept questioning.

Then suddenly, between my eyebrows, area, and a little up, I felt pressure.

I looked at him and said, "What is happening?"

He looked puzzled, and said, "What?"

But the pressure was increasing! It got stronger!!!!

And suddenly, as I was looking at him for help, was magnified the Lord Christ! Just in front of his face, I saw the Lord Jesus! The same magnifying that had happened when I saw the face of Christ, the first time!

I jumped straight up in the air and started screaming and screaming! I fell to the floor and hid my face! Sobbing. Just screaming and crying, out loud, "Oh my God! Oh my God!"

Evangelos leaned down and put his hand on my shoulder and said, "It's alright. We will leave now.

He paid the bill and we walked out. He said, "what would you like to do now?"

I was in shock, but said, "let's get an ice cream cone". So we did.

I sat in the car, still speechless. I watched him as he walked into the shop. I watched as he ordered and paid the money for the cones.

Suddenly, just for a flash, I saw a spirit in him, as he looked at the girl behind the counter! The spirit was a spirit of lust. Looking at the young girl, in a grotesque smile. It was ugly and smirking at the girl! Then it was gone. I never spoke of the spirit to him. I would wait.

47

He gave me my ice cream cone and we talked of his students. They would come with him. He had many students. I never spoke of what I saw, of the Lord magnified, and did not tell anyone.

Chapter Eight

Leaving the Mountains

The whole building had to be cleaned, top to bottom. The students came with lots of energy and supplies to clean it up! I pretty much stayed out of their way. I was living near by and spent very little time during the cleanup. But I did try. They did not want me around! They actually called Evangelos and told him so! His most devoted students did not like me!

But he told them "They would go, before she would go". Meaning me!!!

So for the time being, the students were tolerant of me. They came only on the weekends for seminars. I did try to help as much as I could, with cleaning and such. I watched and tried to do a lot of the exercises. Stretching and yoga. Prayer and meditation and group reading of the Bible.

Our teacher and leader was very advanced and had spiritual knowledge and experience. I greatly enjoyed helping him and being quick to lend a hand. His wife was just the sweetest person. Very beautiful. Their whole family began to arrive more and more frequently as time passed. Then the days increased, that the whole group would stay. Not just the weekends, but four to five days a week, now.

So it was decided that almost everyone would move in. Full time if they could. Over time there was peace between all the other students and me. All conflict had passed. It was a wonderful time of learning and getting healthy. I was working part time, still in the Palo Alto area, at the attorney's office. So I decided to give up the small cottage and

49

move into the Meditation center like everyone else that was involved. We got up very, very early to the sound of a big Bell! Prayer and then exercise and yoga. It was great for me that our teacher was such a Christian. There was no conflict in our beliefs.

The work was hard, physically, to keep the huge lodge running smooth. We dropped trees for fire wood. Almost dropped a tree on the house! We didn't know anything about cutting trees!

My friend from Bridge Mountain wanted to become a student and move in. I didn't interfere with his plan. He was the one that would act like a madman if I was not in his presence. But I thought perhaps that had passed? He seemed alright as time went by. But one day, I was late to the Bible study and reading. I came up the tiny winding staircase and I could hear him reading the Bible to all the students and teacher. As I came closer, my chest and heart area had pains. As though knives were stabbing me. So I stopped and peeked around the corner. I could see him, my friend, reading the Bible. But the sound of it was grotesque! It was read with hatred and anger and was hurting me! I couldn't get any closer and I went downstairs until class was over.

I tried to tell the teacher that I heard evil and that it was hurtful. I related everything that I felt and heard to my teacher.

But he said, "No. I think he will be fine. It was just his way of expressing himself. No harm will come of it."

It was forgotten.

I told my teacher, in the months that followed, that I would be going away, to my family's.

I planned an extended visit with my son and my family. It was summer vacation and I was excited to go!

My teacher would always say, "Until I see your eyes again" —and I would leave him. He knew that many, many times, I barely made it back to him.

And so I said, "Good bye."

My time with my son and family was wonderful. I decided to get an apartment close to my sister and move my son back in with me. I had lived in the same apartment building a few years before. It was clean and comfortable and had a pool. My family was very happy that I would be close by.

So I wanted to tell my teacher, in person, that I would be leaving the North Star Center. I made the long drive south, to the Santa Cruz mountains.

I drove up the long drive to the Lodge, but didn't see anyone! So I walked back to the owners' home.

"Where is everyone," I asked?

They told me that shortly after I left, my friend, that acted crazy when I wasn't with him, went mad! He tore up everything he could get his hands on! Threatened people! Thew furniture and broke furniture! Threw furniture at people! It was a mad house! And my wonderful, gentle teacher, walked away with all his students. He had moved back to San Jose. I felt terrible and responsible for what happened. I knew it was over, for me, too. I had to leave this wonderful place. The place I had been sent to.

I said, "good bye" to the owners of the property. I told them I would probably never return. I somehow knew that this part of my life was over. I never saw them again.

So I drove away. I was well and confident, and happy to make my plans with my son.

We moved into the small apartment near my sister. Actually, the same apartment that I had lived in four years earlier. We moved in and I found a good job. While a great amount of healing had taken place in me, I still seemed very fragile. I would not learn or understand the depth of my wounds and injuries for another 45 years. I had to live through it, slowly, in time, so that I would understand the depth and way back to wholeness. It is explained later, in the end of this book. So my son and I worked at getting along. Getting through his anger for me and at me, for not being there for him and helping him.

But I knew the truth now, about myself and how lost I had been. I wasn't going to give up. Never! It was good to have family so close and we were with them most of the time.

After about a year of many trials and errors, my friend Michael, from my past, found me. I had known him at the time that I left my husband. He was dating the girl I moved in with and was there when my son was born. We had been great friends and he was always kind and quick to lend a hand with my new baby. I always felt he was perhaps the nicest person that I would ever come to know! But we had lost Touch. He had married and had two small children, a boy 5 and a girl 8. Now he was going through a divorce. We went to meet his ex-wife and the children. We took my son and his children and went to Marine World. It was great! I had been employed as a counselor for at risk children. My years in the mountains with the very young, runaways and their drug use, gave me a compassion for the "at risk". I was good at my job. I felt confident in meeting Michael's children. And they did seem to be OK with me.

So we began to see more and more of each other. We both had property, acreage in the wine country. But his wife had just sold their home out from under him! We would picnic and take all the kids to the St. Helena wine country property. I was growing deeply attached to him. Falling in love!

One evening his wife asked to meet me at a nightclub. I went and met her. She said she was going to be direct with me. She liked me. She felt I would be a good influence on her children and wanted to know if Michael and I were serious?

I said, "Yes, we certainly were!"

So she asked, "Will you take my children and raise them if you two are together?"

I looked at her in amazement and saw that she was serious! She said she was ill and again she asked. "Would I be willing to take the children? Michael will be working. You will be the one they will spend their time with. You will be the one to raise them."

Within a few months we did have his two children. We ran off to Reno and got married. We bought a newly built, four bedroom, very large home. So almost overnight we had a large family. Then we had a new son in 1972 and a daughter in 1975.

It was like a whirlwind! We kept my oldest son with us as much as possible. He was having problems during teenage years. It was a busy and full life with such great demands on us as parents. But I ran a tight ship and kept order. My step children really loved their mother, but she would not take them. Although she did spend weekends with them each month. There was conflict. But they did what I said and there was order in the home. I taught Sunday School and we had a large circle of friends and family. Thanksgiving was at our house and it was huge and fun! We had family reunions with generations of family!

So when our youngest daughter became seriously ill, we were devastated. She was four and we went to doctor after doctor, trying to find what was wrong with her.

Chapter Nine

Michael's Beginning of Seeing in The Spirit

My aunt came to visit us. She was the wife of my mother's brother. So, she was my aunt, but not by blood. By marriage. She took my sister at birth and raised her until my father brought my sister home, when I was about five.

So this Sunday, we were all off to church. But our youngest son wanted to stay home with my aunt, for the morning. I said OK and off the rest of us went.

When I got home my son started telling me about other gods and far out stuff! I was upset because I had taken my aunt to church with us the week before and had discussed things with her. I went over that we were Christian in our beliefs and raised the children that way. She had been raised a Christian. So we had discussed our differences and I just did not want her to share any goofy stuff with my kids!

She left a few days later and we talked it all over with all the kids. We laughed about how far out she was and some of the beliefs she had. So we just giggled and were fooling around.

I said, "Well, watch this, I'm going to throw a ball of light to you!"

And so I made my hands go toward each other, fast, like clapping, but not touching! As though I was making energy. And I threw a make believe ball of light or energy at my son!

"Catch!"

He said, "I felt that!"

No!

"Do it again!"

So we started making energy balls and throwing them at each other!

I said to my husband, "I know we can't see it, but how can we feel it? Close your eyes and see if you can see it?"

He closed his eyes, while I made a ball and threw it at my son.

In that moment, our lives were changed forever.

He said, "I saw the ball of energy. You are making a ball of energy and throwing it and I can see it!"

"No!"

It was just crazy! I told him to look more, with his eyes closed. It all happened so fast.

He was seeing in Kirlian photo after image! Everything alive was giving an after image. I think that is what it is?

I tried to keep notes. I did as many drawings as I could. As fast as I could. I have almost everything to go into this book.

What he saw was at first energy fields around each person. With energy affected by emotions and feelings. I had temper fit and was so angry at one of the children.

I told my husband that I was hurting in the chest area and to look at me. I was black throughout my chest. I have never allowed myself to do that again.

At this time my daughter was going to a urologist. She was repeatedly hospitalized with high, high temps. So I asked my husband to look at her. He would tell me what he saw and I did drawings. The urologist said that she had to have surgery. She had very serious kidney disease I needed a second opinion. So we took her to Stanford. After many, many tests, it was confirmed that our urologist was right and we were sent back to him.

Her ureters were re-implanted and other work was done. Our urologist saved her life. And I kept drawings as my husband would look and tell me the colors as she healed.

54

By five and a half, she was almost completely well. We were watching close now and we knew the colors of getting well.

She caught a bad cold. I went to wake her for school. As I leaned over I could smell the "sweet breath" that I had been warned of. I tested her and she was in keto-acidosis. Spilling sugar. I raced her to the hospital and they said she was in a diabetic state and needed insulin. I refused. Just give me time. A little time. If she doesn't come out of it, then we will give her insulin.

What I had recorded, in the days earlier, was the colors of her pancreas getting darker and darker. The cold she had was strep, and I knew by my drawings that it was in her pancreas. But I couldn't tell anyone!

But I was right!!! She completely recovered. Thank God we did not take the insulin!

So for follow up care, we saw her urologist. He was pleased with her recovery. As we were saying "good bye" she turned around and looked at him.

She said, "Don't worry about me anymore, my daddy can see inside me. I am almost a very light green. Like white or yellow! I am almost well!"

A wave of fear came over me and there was no way to hide my shock!

I just walked out. But we would be more careful now.

I realized that to have such a gift as my husband did, that it was a responsibility to help. Especially little children. He could see inside them and if we got the colors right, perhaps we could help. My cousin is a doctor at Stanford and he might have some ideas. So the next time the family was together, we took him aside. We told him about my husband's gift to see. We explained that it was in Kirlian photo after image. That he would be willing to help, with looking at a child or anything when needed? We just wanted to offer our help.

Well he got angry at us! He felt he was insulted! We were worried that we had broken our friendship with him. We had broken the trust he had in us! We were hurt and worried.

So we became very selective on anyone that might find out.

My younger sister got cancer. A very advanced case. She had been put off by doctors and the tumor was the size of a peach. They told her it was nothing to worry about for seven years.

I asked her to let us look at the tumor. I told her the truth about the Kirlian after

55

image. So she agreed.

The breast area of the tumor was purple. Almost black, purple. To her left chest area were black and white squares, then dark purple again. I drew it and recorded it.

The cancer had spread to all of her lymph nodes in the left under arm. They expected her to die. But she did not die. She did get an implant after breast removal. Thirty five years later, it leaked and she did not know it was silicone instead of saline. She had it removed and a new cancer was spread over the entire chest wall. She is still fighting it.

So we thought cancer was purple or black. Infection was dark, almost black and would get lighter and lighter as infection decreased. To dark green, then to lighter and lighter green and then yellow. Eventually the body as it heals is white energy or clear.

I had a lump in the same area as my sister. But it was just gray. So we assumed that it was nothing. We watched it for almost 35 years. It is later explained in this book.

Huge circle as an aura. Just seen once.

56

Chapter Ten

Angels Encounter of Writing This Book

I will try to put the drawings and dates into this book, at the end.

We found and logged all the colors of my daughter after surgery. As the ureters healed and as they became less inflamed. They did return to normal color. The kidneys did return to normal colors. But the kidneys were very damaged and one was small. But an infection returned to the lower bladder area. We took her back to the surgeon. We had to tell him a little bit about my husband, seeing with his eyes closed. He tested my daughter and indeed, she did have an infection. This happened two more times in the next year. Her surgeon did not argue with us when we would return to him. But it was never discussed. He just trusted us now. My daughter did get well.

I will start with the head.

We all have an aura. In a state of well being, the aura is white blue. It is about 4, 5, or 6 inches around the head and whole body. It is over the entire body. Almost as a thick skin of energy or thick coating. The aura will spark something like an ark if you Touch another persons finger tip or almost Touch another person's finger or skin. The aura is largest around the head and shoulders. It has been as big as twenty feet or so, just once, when I was pulling weeds and gardening.

We asked at the end of this book, "why was it so huge?" The "Touch" revealed:

"NATURE"

So I will assume that being outside in nature is very energizing to the being.

There is a halo above each person. At least the ones we have checked.   The halo shifts very slightly with spiritual experience or emotional experience. The halo will darken with stress, illness or all positive and negative influence. To this day, after a lifetime, my halo is dark sometimes when I wake up. This I attribute to subconscious trauma as a baby. It's OK, because it goes away after I get going.

So the halo is a great indicator of the state of the person. Prayer, meditation, uplifting sounds, gardening or many, many things can bring well being and light energy back to the halo and aura. Before my father passed on, we looked at him. His halo had fallen down to his neck area and was dark. He was 95 and passed peacefully.

In a very, very high state of spiritual energy, was seen spokes coming out of the halo. Once, was seen, a second type of halo around the forehead.

Around the shoulders the aura can widen in a high energy state. The aura can have layers of different colors, depending on health and emotional well being. The size changes daily, depending on each person's state of being.

In checking me, my husband found that to my left side was a light. I kept insisting that he try to look more!

He said, "It's an angel!"

"No!"

So I moved across the room. "Look now and keep watching me!"

He did and saw that my angel never moved away from me! Always next to my left side! So we began to look and try harder to see if everyone had an angel! Sure enough, each person has an angel!

But, the position of the angel can be different! One of my sons has the angel right in front of him, in his face! This continued throughout his teenage years!

This is the most significant angel confirmation, issue. I was sitting at the dining room table.

I said to my husband, "Do you think I should be keeping a record of everything that you can see? Everything that we know? My drawings? And perhaps I should write a book?"

All of a sudden my nose and face were vibrating!

I yelled, "Oh my gosh! Something is happening to me! Take a look! Take a look and see what is going on!?"

He said, "It's huge! It has opened its wings! It is stretching and covering you with its wings! It must be a ten or twelve feet across to the tip of its wings! Maybe more!"

I jumped up and ran to the other side of the room!

"What does it want"

He looked.

The angel, with wings still outstretched, reached for me with one hand extended! In the hand was a scepter!

We did not know what it meant. My husband did a drawing of what he saw. It will be in the end of this book.

(Thirty two years have passed. I do know what it means now! I was to take the authority, to write this book!) "To lead' —But I do not know what or anything to lead yet?)

At least I kept notes and drawings and my memory is perfect. We have never seen an angel do this again. We asked at the end of this book, "do angels ever open their wings? The "Touch" revealed:

"RARELY"

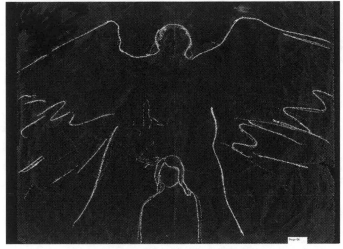

Angel opened wings about this book.

59

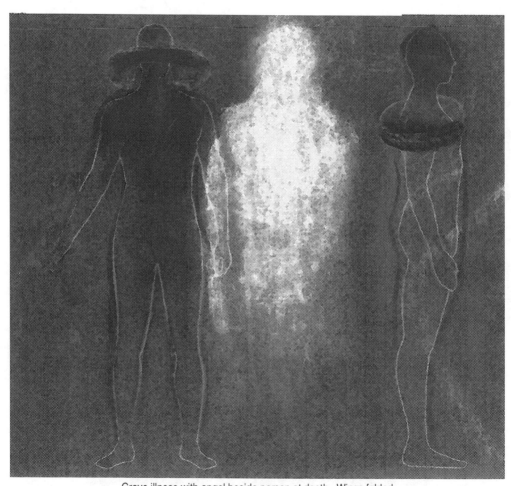

Grave illness with angel beside person at death. Wings folded.

Chapter Eleven

Michael's Lessons About Seeing

I had a friend visit from San Jose. A student from the meditation center. While visiting we told him about my husband being able to see in Kirlian after image. My husband and I are both artists and my friends mother was an artist too. I was familiar with her work. So we planned a visit. It was Christmas time Marin County had wonderful light displays! So we took the kids along. His mother had cookies and snacks for everyone. After looking at her paintings, her son told her about my husband's gift.

She said, "Well, I am a nurse and I just don't believe in such a thing"

Her son insisted that we look at his mom. So against my better judgment, I persuaded my husband to look at her.

He told her that he saw that her aura was good and explained the colors. Then he told her, "that she must have fallen or sustained an injury to her upper arm. He pointed out to her where the line of the injury was.

Well, she got so upset! Then angry and said that her son must have told him that she fell off the roof! She wanted us to leave. It was so awful and hard on my husband, who was so sensitive about this issue! He was angry at me for pushing him to look at her!

I made more of an effort to keep people from asking him to look at them. But I went on with my record keeping and drawings of what my husband would see. I learned what was hurtful to me, or anyone! Anger or a temper fit would make my chest area black! My head black! I began to fast and pray. The family continued on with membership at our local Baptist church. I was still the Sunday school teacher. But I felt a growing need to find a spirit filled church. So we tried the Assembly of God.

The whole family joined Sunday School classes and we enjoyed everyone. The services were moving and the music great! Great singing.

The pastor announce that a group was coming on Saturday night, to sing for us. They were a traveling group. They devoted a six month period to the singing ministry. They had buses and traveled from town to town. They would be housed by congregation members at their scheduled stops.

We decided to take the whole family. The singing was glorious! Very loud and earth shaking! This was a very large group of singers. I think they had three or four buses of singers!

Michael told me, when we got home, late that night, that he saw, way up high, as though there was not a ceiling on this huge church, the Dove, Holy Spirit! It was as big as the entire building. Which was four stories high! Its wings were open and moving. He could hear the sound of the moving wings! So he could see it and hear it!

We have come to learn in the next 35 years how we believe this works.

The word of God says that "God inhabits praise".

This is absolutely true. Praise music brings an outpouring of the Presence of God. Praise in prayer or praise in music, brings God. It's like saying "Hello, I love you", and God says "Hello" back.

It's powerful and earth shaking!

We continued to go to church there. But people were not friendly. So I decided to see if this was my imagination. So after service, I would hurry out and sit outside the door, next to a garden planter box. No one ever stopped or spoke to me, or smiled at me. So I sat there week after week, after each service.

I liked the pastor, so I went to him and told him what I was doing. He was shocked! He told the congregation. He didn't say it was me. He devised a method of having dinners once a month. Potluck. Six families would meet and get to know each other. Everybody would switch the next month. It was fun. And they were friendly and nice!

I began to be aware of a gift or knowledge I had. As a person passed by me, just once in a while, it would be as though a wave of clear glass or a transparency would pass over them. And a knowledge of an injury or hurt would very, very gently come to my mind. In my spirit, if I was led to go further, I would take their hand.

I did help two people. I just mentioned them going to the pastor for prayer and healing of that particular wound.

While going to this church, my oldest son had a wonderful girlfriend. She was living with me after they moved from Los Angeles. She wanted to become a Christian. So one day she asked me if I would help her to understand what is involved? I explained everything that I had learned of how it works. You are sorry for your sins and asked the Lord to be your Savior and you believe that He is the risen Son of God. I think that's it? So we decided we would try it! On our knees, I led her in prayer of how I thought other people did it.

She was so happy and had a profound experience! She did move away and started going to church.

However, something was wrong with me! I felt as though my head was being squeezed!

My husband prayed over me! I went to the church and the pastor prayed over me! I went back to the church and asked for all the pastors to pray over me! Still didn't work. Something was wrong with my head! And it was hurting my head! And I was beginning to be fearful, because no one could help me. And perhaps they were growing tired of me and did not believe me?

I heard about an evangelist or prophet, that was going to be in a town about an hour away. I asked a friend to come with me, since it was at night and a long way away. We arrived late and sat way in the back. Lucky we even got seats, as it was packed with at least 1800 or so people. The sliding and movable walls were opened up to seat the crowd!

The small, frail man came to the stage. He told a little about himself. He was a prophet that was very, very old now.

He stopped speaking and was just looking. He said, "you, with the circles on your shirt, stand up."

I slid down in the seat, almost laying down. I had big circles on my leather shirt, vest!

He said, "I can still see you! You know who you are! Stand up!"

He said, "Your head is being squeezed! You want that demon off your head. You must declare, you want that off your head!"

63

So I said, "I want it off my head!"

He told the crowd to look at me, which they were already doing!

"All of you pray and I will demand!" he said.

"He demanded that it get off my head and leave me alone and never bother me again! He demanded again, "In the name of Jesus Christ!"

He said, "It could not get in you, it was pressing your head"

Later, after the lecture was over, he asked me to stand again. "How do you feel?" he asked?

I said "great!"

"Then thank God" he said, "It's gone!"

I mention this as a lesson. I did not know I was vulnerable to attack if praying someone through!

We continued on as members of the large Assembly of God Church. Then one day, the pastors secretary walked in front of me. Just passed by. She was a very attractive woman. As she passed, the wavy glass like image passed.

Deep inside me I heard the voice of the Lord say, "She will bring this church down. It will be split apart."

I knew that no one would believe me. There was nothing I could do. I told my husband that we were going to leave the church and find one closer to our home. I told him what I had seen and the words I heard. We did not go back. I heard from friends that it did, in fact, fall apart. And that she was, indeed, the cause.

I have learned over the years, that this particular gift, only happens once in a while. It happens only within a church body, when there is a specific need. I don't make it happen. I can't make it happen.

We joined another Baptist church and I started teaching Sunday School again. Life was hard with the step kids, not liking me. I tried to keep my temper under control. A lot of time was extended toward my oldest son. The damage to him in the beginning of his life was taking its toll on him. There was so much conflict within the family. A broken family. But I fasted and prayed more. Tried harder to hold it all together. I read more and more. Listened to the Bible on tapes. Joined small bible studies. All knowledge helped. I studied other religions. Some things good and some things missed the mark!

I understood and saw some of their spiritual flaws and some miss-guided rules.

Our looking at people and the spirit was a very quiet study now. A Touch to the forehead could reveal different lives. Lives from another time period. Old clothes from another time. Perhaps they were my ancestors? Perhaps in my DNA? Perhaps it was me? The present problems and all the needs of my family were what was important! It would be a side track to get into other lives. Frivolous and trivial, compared to the present need and attentiveness!

When I was researching a book on my family, as they came across the planes, in wagon trains, that girl was in my head. Or she showed in my head? She was an Indian, watching the wagon train. Then she was hiding in the tall grass, with a baby in her arms. Hiding from soldiers. Then I would be seen with my oldest son, playing, as we walked in the woods. Now, it could have been my ancestors? One that looked like me? I don't know and I don't think this is a very important piece of the puzzle? We are connected to our past, perhaps sometimes there can be quite an influence on this present life. An ache in the heart. A fear? But that would have to be another book.

This book is about the present life and the aura and the spiritual, present, unseen life!

So as we continued on, in the search of what it all meant, we learned a lot.

The greatest damage is done by one's anger. Anger can make the chest or head area go from white to black, in a few moments. This was the greatest thrust of our study and trying to learn what happens with anger. The greatest power is the power of forgiveness!

You are set free. You have to work at it and say it out loud. Your brain has to hear your own voice.

So, if asked, my husband would look at a person. I would draw their aura and try to color it quickly. Then we would tell them as much as we knew, from past colors, what might be wrong or right. Telling each person about their halo. The halo is the tell all of how you are doing. So much so that we look there first for the health and spiritual well being of the person.

We did not know at this time that dark gray was cancer. As we were watching my gray spot and were not aware. My sister's cancer area was black purple and black, so we thought only black was cancer. The cancer had spread to all my sister's lymph nodes and she was given only a 20% chance of survival. We are so close and this was a very hard time. We talked about the Lord and our belief in God.

So, again, if my husband looked at a person, everything could be read in the aura. But, if he "touched" them with the right hand on the head top or forehead, lives could be seen. Lives from another time. Sometimes it was in the present.

The spiritual world is inter woven with the mind and body. At the end of this book I will give my conclusion. Complete and leave no question.

We were going through hard years at this time. With five teenage kids, the needs were huge! There were a lot of problems with such a broken family. We were the broken family of his, mine and ours, children, family. Divorce is so hard on children and losing a parent to divorce.

We did check everyone that came into our presence to see if they had an angel. Every person did. This is absolute fact. The angel is normally on the left. Almost never would the wings be open! But, as I said earlier, we saw it in front of one of our children. Almost nose to nose as if trying to block? My angel reached for me only once, as mentioned earlier in this book.

One of our sons, in Junior High, had a friend over for the night. I knew the boy's family and liked them. We all went to bed. Perhaps around 1 am the boy got up, as he couldn't sleep. The next day, he related to my son, that he was looking out our living room window. Just thinking about walking home because he couldn't sleep. As he sat looking out in the dark, he began to hear mocking, scary voices! They were saying, "Jesus, Jesus".

Over and over, again, Mocking and telling him to come out! They were yelling at him through the glass! He told my son that it was terrifying!

And I felt assured, that within our home, we were doing all we knew, to keep evil out!

But a few months later, we had another incident.

One of our son's girlfriends came over for a visit. I was in the back of the house sewing. She came in and sat down near me. She told me all of her troubles, while away at college. She had some very frightening experiences at her parents home, during her last visit. She felt she had been drugged at college and used in some kind of ritual. But had no memory of the details of the incident. She had a very isolated and protective childhood on her families farm. A soft spoken country girl and very likeable. She was very troubled spiritually and asking me for help.

I began to tell her about the Bible. That it was actually the Living Word of God! That it was alive. If she would read it and take it into her heart, she would find help! We had a Bible right there and I could have read a line or two, to her. She did believe me and listened attentively.

All of a sudden, my husband appeared in the doorway. With a bit of anger in his voice, he said, "What are you doing? I think it's time for her to go home. It's getting late!"

What a strange thing for my husband to do! But I said "Good night" and walked her to the door.

With the door closed and she was out of sight, I asked, "What was that all about?"

Again he asked, "what were we doing?"

I told him that I was just telling her how to read the Bible. "That it was the Living Word of God".

"She believed me and took it into her heart", I told him.

"What's wrong?" I asked again!

So he explained to me what had happened. He said:

"While you were in the back of the house, talking, little demons came out into the living room, where I was sitting. They came in at lightning speed! They were small and looked like little swine. Perhaps five or six in number! They were spinning in a large circle in the middle of the living room! Whirling around in a large circle so fast, that I could barely see them! Then they flew out the front door!! Perhaps after her? But they could not stay in the house!"

He told me he was very surprised and concerned!

While I never saw this young woman again, I did talk with her on the phone. We got into a heated discussion. I did not tell her what we saw, but I told her she needed help. She needed to join a spirit filled church. She needed counseling and prayer! I knew it was not me, that would be able to help her!

Chapter Twelve

Warfare and Battles in The Spirit

A few months passed. My step daughter got married. A large wedding. My stepson was visiting his mother for the summer. Things were quiet at home. We were saying "good night" to the two youngest teenagers. We always said the Lord's Prayer with them and said "Good night".

As we were praying with our son, he said that he was getting pains in the heart area and the chest and stomach! At the same time, I heard, as clear as clear can be, the voice of the Lord, say:

"GET ANY OIL AND PRAY OVER YOUR SON!"

So I yelled at my husband, "Stop praying! I have to get oil and we have to pray over him!"

I ran and found oil and brought it to my husband as fast as I could! I was scared! My husband looked at me, a little annoyed!

He took the oil and anointed our son's forehead. He began to pray out loud! Demanding and rebuking anything to come out of him or off him! But as he prayed, I noticed he became louder and louder and more demanding!

I just followed along, in prayer, not knowing what was happening?

Finally my husband stopped praying. We were all quiet and waiting. Very slowly and very deliberate, my husband related what happened!

When he prayed and anointed our son with oil, the demon started to come out! My husband could see it. It was big, huge! He said it looked like a domestic cat, but a head as big as a lion. Grotesque and misshapen! Monstrous! Perhaps 7 or 8 feet tall! As he demanded and declared it get out, it began to disintegrate and got smaller and smaller and left! With a poof!

It was gone. Our son didn't have any more symptoms of pain, while we prayed over him, again. I suppose we brought it in, probably in stray cats, that we were always adopting and finding homes for.

While I could not see in the spirit, I did, just once, see something.

I had gone with the first grade class to an evening open house. It was Halloween and the kids had made a fun house at the school. We walked over, as it was just a block away. Everything was decorated and very scary. Fortune tellers, haunted houses and everything imaginable for a huge Halloween open house! But I was uneasy walking through? I couldn't wait for the kids to all have their fill of the place and we could get out? But they wanted to see everything. Finally we were on our way home and did a little trick or treating. It had been a fun evening.

During the middle of the night, I woke with a start! My eyes opened to see the silhouette of two figures battling. Arched and noses almost touching in fierce combat! They disappeared as soon as I was fully awake! They knew I saw them. It was my angel battling furiously for me! I had gone into the enemy territory and was fair game! I vowed to not participate in Halloween again. I had done nothing but walk through the building. But it was taken in the spirit world that I was a participate. I was fair game! I will always remember the fury of the fight for me! I will add a drawing of it to this book.

And on the same subject, I will tell what happened to my nephew, Bill and his wife.

He was a hard working young man. A heavy drinker and pretty wild! Loved to fight and rough it up! But one morning, while in the shower, the Lord spoke to him.

He said,

"I WANT YOU TO DEVOTE YOUR LIFE TO ME."

Well, I was the first person he ran to! I was miss goody two shoes! I went to Church, so he came to me. But I didn't know what to say or what to think? I didn't give any advice.

But within a week or so, I had a dream. In the dream, I was walking with the Lord. Through long open expanse of grassy fields. It was wonderful just walking with the Lord. Then He spoke. He said:

"I WANT HIM. I WANT ALL OF HIM. HIS LIFE"

Well you can be sure that I ran to tell him! First thing in the morning! I told him, word for word, what the Lord said about him in my dream!

Bill was shocked. He joined a church, became very active and became a deacon. He started classes to become a minister. He was happy and all seemed to be going well.

They moved away and he became a full time building contractor. Perhaps the work was all consuming. Who knows what happened. He fell away and started drinking and partying. Having a grand old time!

A short time passed. All of our family knew he was drinking and partying again. We left him alone and did not criticize him. Then one day, he was there at my door. He came in, with his wife and sat down.

He said, "I have something to tell you. We woke up early one morning, last week. The Lord spoke to me and said, "You want the world. I will show you what is in the world. I will open your eyes"

And with that, Bill could see into the spirit world. He said there were demons all over the place! They were grotesque! Hiding and peering out from behind anything! They were behind everything! He woke his wife up to help him! But she could see them too! She was scared to death. She hid under the blankets in bed. They were terrified! It lasted almost an hour? He begged forgiveness and would turn his life around! He came to see me to tell me he was going into full time ministry.

He did become a minister to the homeless and rescue missionary work. He never faltered again in his life. He just needed that wake up call!

We began to plan for our retirement. We sold our home and rented for three years as we built our small home in the country. I forgot about the book. This book.

We moved to a small fishing village called Bodega Bay. Next to an Artist Community! It was great to meet them all and I got a part time job in a Gallery. I was good at selling paintings!

We were busy painting and getting our paintings into galleries. We were selling our paintings and enjoying the excitement of showing.

Then I began to get weak. I seemed to have a gray color in my face.

71

I was checked by doctors and they came up with nothing? I had ultrasounds. The lump in my breast, that we had been watching for years, was seen clearly. They told me not to worry about it. It was nothing to worry about. Even though my family had a history of cancer. Even though I told them about my sister having cancer.

"Don't worry". It is nothing. So I didn't worry. I had all the tests that would surely show if I had any problems?

Chapter Thirteen

Cancer Revealed

At an antique doll show in San Rafael, California, in late October, 1997, I picked up five antique doll heads. Each had a tiny hairline fracture. Some were in the back of the head and invisible. What a deal, I thought, only $100 and I had some antique bodies packed away at home. I was just guessing at sizes, but I knew they were close. Being in the business of antique doll repair, I knew they would be beautiful when I was finished with each one.

I waited about two weeks, then started looking through the cupboards in our garage apartment. I couldn't find the box with the large body in it. I had a 26-inch doll body in there somewhere! One more place to look. I called to my husband to help me move furniture away from the wall where a panel opened to storage, under an eve overhang. He said he'd be there in a minute. I waited a few minutes, then thought I could get started. I'm really strong. I tried but I was pulling furniture across carpet, Berber carpet, and it was hung up! I crouched down and pulled the furniture toward me. Nothing. So I pulled and pulled and my arms and hands were close together and I heard and felt a snap, snap, snap in my chest! I did move the piece of furniture. I looked in the cupboard, found the doll body, left the room, and went down the stairs. I left the apartment and walked over to the main house. Within a few hours I knew I had hurt myself. I could only lay on the couch and roll off straight on to the floor. I thought I hurt my back and that the pain in my chest was from nerves connected to my back or perhaps a disc?

I laid on ice packs and kept them in the area between my shoulders. I was unable to get in and out of bed. I could only roll off of the bed to my knees. My family helped me to get on my feet and to lie down. I told them that I would go to the doctor within a few days if I didn't get better. I didn't want to be one of those cases that by the time you get to the doctor, you're feeling OK. I thought my body would heal itself. But I didn't get better.

I got much worse in the next two weeks.

On November 17th I called our family doctor's office and asked if I could come right in. They said, no, they were too busy. Four to five doctors in this small medical center and I had seen most of them on previous visits, as well as the nurse practitioner.

I said "I could be having a heart attack and I can't breath".

"That is too bad. We are just too busy... Go to the local emergency room," the girl said.

I told her I would check to see if another doctor in town, Dr. Belvin, could see me. We had met him once while he was covering for another doctor. I called and he said to come right in. I called the clinic right back and asked if I could have a copy of my last blood work, so that this new doctor wouldn't have to do blood work over again. When I arrived at the office, there was no copy, but my complete file was on the counter.

They didn't care. They didn't want to be bothered. The nurse practitioner had told me that perhaps I should see a psychiatrist! That there was nothing wrong with me! What an insult! I just took the file and left without a word.

Dr. Belvin gave me a complete physical. I couldn't move my arms. Any movement in the shoulder and chest area was unbearable.

The doctor said that I probably pulled the muscles in my chest and that it could be quite painful and may take a long time to heal. He gave me strong pain pills and an anti-inflammatory. He sent me home and I tried to cope with the pain.

My husband was looking at my chest area now. We would check it each day. He could see that it was gray. The sternum area was gray. Of course we thought cancer was purple and black. So we thought my back was out. But my sternum seemed to be getting bigger? It was very slightly starting to protrude?

Two weeks passed, the pain worsened and I asked to be rechecked. Dr. Belvin said it must be the muscle pain, but scheduled X-rays. On December 1, 1997, my first x-ray was done. The report was negative. Nothing showed. Chest x-rays were done to rule out TB or pneumonia.

Within a week I couldn't move my chest area or arms. I called Dr. Belvin and was rechecked on Dec. 8. He did an EKG thinking the pain might be from the heart. Nothing showed.

Thinking still, that my back was out, I called a local chiropractor, who was highly recommended. I told him the story of what I had been through. One arm couldn't be moved and the pain in my chest was unbearable. He said he wouldn't Touch me with a ten-foot pole! He ordered special X-rays that would determine if any bones were broken. The reports were again negative. Nothing.

I was put on stronger pain medication.

The gallery that showed my paintings and my husband's paintings, asked me to work. They wanted me to fill in because the owner had breast cancer. She needed a lot of time off. With the new pain pills, I would be able to just sit at the gallery and not exert myself. It is usually slow in the winter. So I did go to work, however it was very busy, with a lot of people coming through. I worked much harder than I had expected. Here I was in this body and could feel what was happening, but all the professionals were telling me I was wrong. That nothing was happening in there!

My health seemed to be slipping. My breathing was much more painful as time went on. I didn't know what to do. The results from the last physical showed on a computer run-off that everything was fine, except a higher risk for cancer because of family history. My sister had cancer, my grandfather, my uncle and my aunt. I had now been checked so many times for cancer and told I was in the clear!

I found that I could double up on the pain medication and get myself to work. The paintings had to be hung and moved. The area in my breast-bone was still showing a slight swelling. The sternum area. Three months had passed now, since I moved the furniture and heard the snaps.

I agreed to organize and promote a group show of six local artist in May of 1998. It meant that I had to get busy and paint. My husband and I would both be in the group show and reception. The gallery owner walked me through how to set up the advertising and the photo work. My Daughter and her fiance helped with the advertising and got it on the radio. They set up a fantastic catering. What a turnout! The show and reception was a great success!

I was very busy at the gallery and trying to get paintings and prints ready to show. Customers liked to meet the artist and it was a lot of fun to show my own work.

I was still very concerned about how I was feeling.

(At this time we did not know anything about the "Touch" with two hands. That would be yet another ten years away. We knew my husband could see in the Kirlian after image. We knew the colors of disease or infection were dark green and yellows. We knew he could "Touch" a person's forehead and see other lives. We had only seen cancer as purple and black.)

But I was weak. I knew something wasn't right. In May 1998 I decided to go to the breast clinic in Santa Rosa, Radiology Medical Group. They did a complete mammogram of both breasts. It was very difficult to take the mammogram because my sternum was growing and they couldn't get me up to the plate for the exam. We couldn't Touch my sternum. We worked around it and completed the exam. I was leaving and said good-bye to the technician, and told her how well my sister is doing since reconstruction.

She said, "Oh you'd better go back and wait. I should tell the radiologist about that."

They brought me back inside for an extensive ultrasound. The radiologist came in and worked on me personally. He identified a mass in my left breast at the 1 o'clock position. He pointed it out. I could see it on the screen.

He said "I don't know what that is, but I'm sure it's nothing to worry about."

"I can see it" I said, "What is it?"

"Well I don't know, but I will review your records and get back to you."

I received a letter in a few days saying it wasn't cancer. He noted in the letter my family history of cancer. I felt relieved and determined to have my spine checked further. My back must be out, I thought.

I continued to work at the gallery until Fourth of July, 98. I was determined that if there was nothing wrong with me, as everyone was insisting, I must continue to work. I was showing and selling my paintings now. And I was selling my husband's paintings in the gallery too! This was such a great opportunity for both, my husband and me. I wanted to will myself out of the downward spiral I was in with my health and seemingly bad luck. I felt that by hanging on to my job and selling my paintings, that I was normal, healthy. Perhaps I would get better if I was busy doing what I liked and I liked selling paintings. But I quit my job because of a frightening experience.

The gallery is situated off Highway One in Bodega Bay. It is apart from the rest of the small village and completely out of view. It was almost closing time and there were two couples on the far side of the gallery, two rooms away from me. My husband was going to pick me up in about 45 minutes. From the front window I saw a large white van pull up. It had a rowboat strapped on the top of it. A blond, very tall man got out and walked up the steps to the gallery. He came into the lobby area and walked right past me into my office. I said that's the office and it is private. He didn't respond to me or speak. He had shorts on and was clean. He looked at me in anger and turned and walked away into another part of the gallery. The hair on my neck was standing straight up. This was trouble. I'm very sensitive and intuitive and all my bells and whistles were going off. I went in the office and started yelling orders to the back room, like I had lots of workers back there. I started slamming doors in the bathroom and making lots of noise. I walked into the entryway to see if I could find which part of the gallery he was in. I saw the other two cars pulling away. I knew we were alone. And he knew it too.

I could see him way back in a corner. His back was to me and he was rocking back and forth and seemed to be talking to himself. He was looking at the floor and rocking and making sounds. Everything in my mind was frozen with the urge to leave the gallery. I was so torn! Run and leave everything! All the cash!? I grabbed the cell phone and went outside. On the deck, I could move around the gallery and see him. But he didn't know where I was.

A voice, inside me, quietly said, "Do not speak to him, do not say one word."

He came out and saw me. I was pretending to water the plants and check them. He started rocking, leaning way back and then way forward. I didn't move or speak or look directly at him.

He went back in the gallery. I called my husband on the cell phone and told him to hurry. But I knew it would be 15 minutes before he could get there. I walked past the entry window and saw him again, way in the corner, rocking. He came back out and stood by the door. Just stood there. I was around the side of the building, looking through two sets of windows at him. He seemed to be angry and talking to himself. He went back in. I walked toward the front of the gallery deck just as he was coming out. He started down the front steps to leave. I knew he was leaving! He was such a huge man!

I made the mistake of speaking! I said "Thank you for stopping in."

Big error on my part! Now I had his attention! He was only a few feet from me now. He started back up the stairs toward me and looked up at me directly. I didn't move or flinch. The sun was shinning on me and he started rocking and talking to himself! He looked at me and I knew my white gray hair was glowing in the sunlight! I knew my hair was saving me! Perhaps it reminded him of someone? Perhaps it was that I was old? He started rocking and swaying again! Then he turned away and walked down the stairs and drove off.

I locked up and watched for my husband. I was scared to death. But he hadn't done anything physically harmful. We didn't have police and what could I have said, "that he rocked and looked scary?"

No, only I would ever know what he was like. I knew that he was hell bent on hurting someone! My intuition was telling me that he intended to kill someone. During the experience it was as though my mind, my physical body and my intuition were one. Operating on a high, very intense level. It was as though a primitive survival mode clicked in. I didn't know at that time, that I was going to be in this mode all the time, very soon! As it turned out, I was right and he was dangerous!

A few day later, over the Fourth of July weekend, my son and a group of his friends came in the gallery, during the parade. I mentioned that I was quitting, because of the isolation of the gallery.

My son said that as he was leaving the gallery after helping me, two days earlier, he heard a voice inside himself say, "Go back. Your mother is going to be killed!"

Of course he thought he was crazy and just kept driving on south. I realized then, that being sensitive to my inner voice had, perhaps saved my life. The experience showed me a part of myself that could protect me, if I would listen. Listen to myself. It is my conclusion about this incident, and the crisis ones that were in my immediate future, could have intervention from a higher authority! God, my spirit, my intuition and my very being, needed to guide me in the coming crisis.

I left my job. I felt bad, but I couldn't get over my fear, that he would come back. The owner did revamp the alarm system and the women had an alarm trigger on their belt. We had always been there alone and at east they believed me.

I was satisfied that I had worked at the gallery long enough for the owner to recuperate from breast surgery. We were all quite concerned about her being able to come back to work after reconstruction surgery. But she did quite well. And she talked and talked about getting a second opinion on a mammogram someplace other than the small country hospital, locally. I told her that I had done that in May of this year. I had taken my previous records, mammograms and ultrasounds from our local hospital and had all comparative mammogram and ultrasound. The radiologist said that the small spot, that was noted in my left breast for the previous four years, was nothing. It was there at the 1 o'clock position, "but it was nothing. Not cancer. He had assured me.

~~~

Three editors, a publisher and most of the initial readers asked me to remove this incident with the scary man that came into the Gallery! "It just seems too extraneous" and not connected, they all told me. Although seemingly unrelated, it is the foundation of my story. This is my experience with survival. Survival is the basis of my story. It was within me to know intuitively what to do to survive. I just needed to tune in and listen when I heard the truth, the truth in my mind and my spirit. In time the truth from my caregivers would save my life. But survival was in my hands, my decision and my choices.

Chapter Fourteen

Knowing Leonard Lake and Charles Ng

As the summer went on, I seemed to be getting weaker and weaker. I decided to go to a new doctor in town, a Dr. Smith. I did and I liked her a lot. I seemed to be run down and weak. I got an infected ear and began to run high temperatures. It appeared to be mastoids and I stayed overnight in the hospital on an IV with antibiotics.

In August "98 the public defenders office from Orange County sent two investigators to my home. They parked outside my gate until they served me with papers to appear as a witness for the defense of Charles Ng! He was going to be tried as a mass murderer! I couldn't believe it! Go all the way to Orange County. I didn't know Ng, had never seen him. At least I didn't remember seeing him? But I had seen his accomplish. Leonard Lake, the mass murderer! I certainly remembered seeing him and his wife! The crimes that are too horrible for me to even think about.

I became involved in this in a very happenstance way. It occurred 1984. We were driving home on Hwy. 128, through Philo. I was with my husband and our two youngest children, eight and ten years old at the time. We stopped at a garage sale. Walked around and looked at items. Cameras, war memorabilia, sewing machines, knives, car parts and tires. Just lots of everything. This young woman walked with me. Very quiet, soft-spoken. I'd ask her about items as we walked and talked.

"How much is this?" She would turn away from me, lower her head and walk over to a very large man. He was in overhauls and a plaid shirt. She would keep doing this. I thought it was strange that she just wouldn't say, "Hey, how much is this?" Just yell! But she didn't. Out of the corner of my eye I could see my little daughter also running over to him. He never moved, not once! He only watched us. We picked out a spare tire for the station wagon, some cameras, some antiques and I asked if she would take a check. She turned, lowered her head and went to him. Came back and said, "yes". I said how should I make it out. She did the same thing, came back and said "cash"

I made the check out to cash and we left.

Within the month, July 1984, the IRS notified me that I was going to be audited. I had to prove all my deductions. In going through my canceled checks, there was the one made to "cash". I thought, maybe we could deduct that spare tire, because we had to drive to the rental property we owned. I turned it over and saw the signature read "Charles Gunnar". I knew that name. It had been on the news. He was one of perhaps 25 or more victims of Leonard Lake and Charles Ng. I quickly looked at the cameras and found a name inside on each. The next day on the SF News they announced that anyone who had bought items at garage sales from these people, should call SF Police Homicide. So I called and Identified myself and gave the homicide detective the two names in the cameras. I gave the name on the back of my check. They thanked me and wanted the check. I said after my audit, I would mail it.

In 1989, now five years later, a detective called after we sold our home and were renting. We had a new phone number and they were keeping track of me! He said they were just checking in? They asked if I would alert them if I moved again! I didn't. I forgot about it! I didn't think much of it as Leonard Lake had killed himself and his wife was a witness for the prosecution. About five more years passed and in 1994 they called again, wanting the check. But after the audit it must have been put in a special place, I can never find anything I put in a special place. They came to Bodega Bay to "just talk" in 1995. I heard nothing until 1998 when I was served to appear as a witness for the defense! I thought it might be the defense of the woman. She was frightened of the man that I now know to be Leonard Lake. I could tell them that, but not much more? But the defense of Ng! I called them up and bawled them all out! They must be hitting the bottom of the barrel if they needed me? I hadn't even seen Ng. I told them I was not well and perhaps not even well enough to travel. I thought it might not even go to trial. No date was set yet. What if I have a temper fit on the stand about how I feel about what happened? Perhaps they will throw me in jail! Everyone was warning me not to speak out, only answer the questions.

By August 1998 I was becoming more ill. It was hardly noticeable. I checked my life insurance small print and really read it. Instead of this great policy I had been sold, over ten years earlier, I had six thousand dollars paid in already. People like me that thought their policy was increasing, but the fees and fines were greater than any growth would ever be. Another company offered a plan to automatically deduct premiums. I signed up. The doctor that had to do the extensive physical was my own Dr. Belvin! I put on the application that I had hurt my chest and rib area. I wrote that I had an EKG and extensive tests. I passed with flying colors!

By this time I was sure I must have a ruptured disk and all the pain and swelling was from the back. I was served papers October 20, 1998 to appear in Orange County on December 2, 1998. I called the public defender and told him how ill I was, but it didn't matter.

I drove to Santa Cruz to visit my father, at 93 years young and tough as nails! I took him shopping and then left for my daughter's home in Rio Del Mar. I stayed for a few days and would take pain meds as soon as I woke up. But I was weaker? We were in a condo on the side of the cliffs with a great view, and very nice location. We're best buddies and have fun shopping. So many things to do and so many shops to go to! There is just never enough time, especially antique and collectors shops in her area! She had said not to carry the basket of laundry down, but she was busy fixing lunch. So I went up the two flights of wooden, outside steps. Very, very carefully I stepped down each step, with the basket of laundry. I got all the way to the bottom. The last step. I was weak and the weight of the basket caused me to lean to the left. My ankle turned under me and I heard a terrible tearing, and then a snap! I called out and tried to crawl into the apartment. My foot was turning purple and swelling. I was getting sick to my stomach. I couldn't stay alert. I kept starting to pass out. A doctor lived above my daughter and she ran to get her. The doctor felt I should go to the hospital. I said OK. I could crawl outside and crawl up the stairs. I made it up two steps and couldn't move and barely stay conscious. I just stayed on my knees.

So they called an ambulance! Fire trucks came with sirens screaming! It was very embarrassing because the staircase was very slim! The attendants couldn't get anything down, to carry me up! I couldn't turn over. They had to turn me right side up. Wrapped my lower leg in ice and made it stiff. One got me under the arms and one got my feet and they carried me up. I did weigh 150 lbs and they said they worked for their money that day. Off we raced in the ambulance to the hospital. My daughter in a car behind us! I fractured the ankle and was put on more pain medication. I stayed the night. Took lots of meds and was off for home in the morning. The brace on my lower leg worked fine.

I saw my attorney when I got home. I explained the fractured ankle and my slipping health. I just couldn't make the trip to Southern California for the trial! But he said I had to go.

"Well, what if I don't?"

He said, "They will put out a bench warrant for you. But I'll call them!"

The Public Defender said I had to be there even if I needed an escort!

So back to my doctor I went. I filled her in on the trial and my broken ankle. I told her I had been busy trying to get a new policy. That my sternum problem hasn't gotten any attention. It was still growing? That I'd had another physical for insurance and I appeared to be just fine. The other doctor insisting it was just a pulled muscle. But

I did declare on the application that I had hurt myself a year ago.

She looked at my sternum and wrote a letter for my attorney. I got a new brace for my ankle. She wrote to my attorney that I could not take a deep breath and that a complete work-up was in progress to identify the swelling of my chest. She suggested that I would be allowed to speak slowly and take time to breathe between questions on the stand.

It was November 24th and my doctor was going on vacation. She was ordering an MRI to be done after the Holidays. So the next day we saw my attorney and we gave him the letter from my doctor. But the request for an attendant was not in writing, just my injuries. He wanted a family member or an attendant to accompany me. He called the Public Defender and said he would try to do everything by fax. I hurried over a few blocks to Dr. Belvin's office. I asked him if he would write a note that my sternum was causing breathing difficulties.

"Why? You're doing just fine"

No! I need an MRI and I'm being asked to travel to a trial and I'm too weak!"

"Well, if you are not better in a few months, we'll think about it" he said.

I left. The next day, Thanksgiving, and everyone was gone until Monday, I began to feel as though I was fighting a hidden enemy? And I wasn't winning! For the first time I felt the stalking of doom! Nothing I did seemed to stop the events from evolving. My attorney didn't even get the call through, let alone a fax. Nothing was done, although I got billed for another $95 from the attorney.

Chapter Fifteen

The Hard Trip to Ng Trial

The trip to the court in Orange County would involve two or three days. I packed just a few items, a small bag, took a large purse and my cell phone. My husband dropped me off at SFO. Late in the afternoon I landed at John Wayne Airport in Santa Ana, asked around and found my way outside to the courtesy pick up area for the Holiday Inn. I called and then waited a half hour. No one showed up? All this time I was lugging around my huge purse stuffed to capacity and a leather small suitcase, stuffed as well. I could feel the pull on my chest as I tried to carry the bags in and out of the airport lobby and then back to the curb to look for my ride. The brace on my ankle was hurting. I was really getting angry! I called the Holiday Inn again, but this time I was yelling mad! It was getting dark and I had already been approached twice. I found out later that the driver was upstairs having coffee. He showed up 45 minutes later!

When I arrived at the Holiday Inn they alerted the Public Defender and his assistants. It was the same two investigators that had waited outside my front gate to serve me. After I unpacked, they escorted me into the conference room to be questioned. Everyone was nice and apologized for making me travel with my medical problems I leaned forward,, across the table, toward Atty. Wm. Kelly, the Public Defender and told him, "I can barely breathe. If I am not there in the morning for you, it is because I have checked myself into a hospital. I am not happy about any of this"!

He said my attorney called him while he was at lunch and didn't call back or fax anything. They would have gladly sent and paid for an attendant. He went on to question me about Leonard Lake and his wife. Photos were shown to me. I related the garage sale, the IRS series of events and then we were finished for the evening.

I was up around 4:30 am December 3, 1998 and packed quickly. Got down to the lobby by 6 and was informed that I would be picked up by Coast Yellow Cab. I'd be driven with another witness to the Santa Ana Superior Court. An hour passed and no Cab! We started calling the taxi company. It was warm outside so I waited in the approach turn about. A cab pulled up from Coast and I told him who I was and could he take us to court, even if it was not his order? He checked with dispatch.

Then he said, "Get in!"

She said we were late! We got our luggage in and were off! He burnt rubber and we were on the Santa Ana Freeway in 30 seconds. I was so concerned about my chest pains, that earlier I had taken ¼ of a beta-blocker, just to be safe. Good thing I did, as he darted in and around cars and trucks, I got more nervous. The heater was going full blast and it was warm outside. He said it was broken and he couldn't turn it off. Inside the cab there was no upholstery on the doors or most of the interior! We were getting thrown all over the back seat. The other woman didn't seem to mind the high speed at which we were going? Well, we missed the turn off! Then to make up time, he really started going faster!

I said, "Where are you from?" Knowing he missed the off ramp!

He said, "Wisconsin. I've been here 30 days!" He had to exit, get back on the freeway, go backwards and get to almost where we started. And he was determined to make the time up.

I couldn't breathe. My left arm started going numb and I couldn't breathe. The pain in my chest was like a sledgehammer hitting me. The lady with me yelled at the driver to take it easy. She yelled at him that I was having a heart attack! I thought, "this is it. I am going to die on the Santa Ana Freeway going in circles with a nut! OK God there is nothing I can do now. He could kill us just trying to get to a hospital and get lost?!

But we got to the DA's office and the other witness didn't want to leave me. I told her I was OK, to go on. My appointment was with the public defender, separate offices and departments.

The court was just a block away. We could see it. He raced over! I got out with my bags and went in to court. In the lobby I told the guards and police that I thought I might be having a heart attack.

They asked, "where are you going?"

"To the Ng trial", I said.

"You must go to the courtroom that you're scheduled to appear in and tell the bailiff!"

"Even though I might be dying, I have to check in"?

"Yes!"

I drug all my bags and myself to the elevator and went in to the courtroom. I saw the bailiff, a lot of police and deputies. I told them I was ill. They sent the DA over to talk to me. He said I would be the first witness and they would get me out as fast as possible. They asked me to put my bags by the rail, sit and rest and wait for the jury to come in. I could overhear two men across the isle from me talking. They were writers, talking about serial killers. I wondered if family members of the victims were here with me? Then I saw the people I knew from the Public defenders office come in. They were talking about giving Ng a clean shirt! A clean shirt! He was covered in other peoples blood! A clean shirt won't do it! So I went out in the hall to sit and wait. A large group of oriental people sat down next to me. They were Ng's family. Seemed very nice people, young. They were all so normal. I hated all of this!

Shortly I was called into court and to the stand. I was pretty settled down by now. I sat within inches of the Judge. But he was about two feet above me and to my left. He was a large man that just looked down at me. And he kept telling me to speak up. The questioning began and I repeated my story. I watched only the public defender as he spoke to me. His gray hair matched his gray suit and he was nice looking.

I thought, "Why is this such a trauma for me? My health?"

And as clear as an audible voice, the voice of the Lord said:

"YOU ARE ALL GROWN UP NOW   THERE IS NOTHING TO
BE AFRAID OF."

The DA started questioning me. A very soft spoken man. As I was looking at him, I realized that everything was similar to the rape trial when I was a little girl. The wound of it matched up in my brain. And it was gone. The fear associated with this trial vanished. It was just similar!

No problems with the DA's questioning. Then I looked over at Ng. His head was down, nearly touching the table in front of him. His body was slumped forward almost in a ball. He was nothing, small and dead.

"His life is over", I thought to myself. He has hurt men, women and children. I was hurt by a person like him! And I have just been set free of another fear and block in my memories!

85

And a major change happened inside of me! I was strong and he was weak! He wouldn't look at me. Finally the questioning was over and I was dismissed. I didn't even turn my head toward the jury.

I left the court and the assistants walked me back to their office to call a cab for the airport. When the cab arrived, the detective leaned in and said to the driver, "Take her to the airport and drive slow and mellow. She had a hair raising trip here this morning."

He turned out to be a good driver and the trip was fine. Got to the airport at 10 am but couldn't get out until 7 pm! The flights were overbooked and they kept bumping people. I was exhausted by the time I got to SFO. Missed the connector flight and had to catch a bus. My chest pain was unbearable.

I was so happy to see my husband waiting for me. Then the long drive up the coast. Past the garage sale parking lot in Philo, where it all began with Leonard Lake. But I explained to my husband that it might have all been worth it! I had the Lord speak to me in the court room and had a memory healed. It was as though I matched it up and it was now understandable. That was good enough for me. Finally we got home and I got some well needed rest.

Chapter Sixteen

Never To Eat Red Meat Again

Through the Christmas Holiday season I began to search for a facility for my open MRI. One that would be within driving distance. I found one five hours away. I couldn't drive that far. One in Santa Rosa was near installation completion. Their appointment secretary gave me the phone number of an open MRI in San Francisco. So I had it done on January 2, 1999.

It was a hard exam even though it was called open! A very long test. The test showed my spine and vertebra normal. But it did show an expansive mass in the body of my sternum. I was shocked. A CT scan and/or bone scan was recommended. I was asked if there had been trauma? Of course there had been, at the time I heard the snap, snap, snap; but that was over a year ago?

So a week later I had a CT scan which diagnosed the mass as a Brodies' abscess in my sternum. It showed three fractured ribs to the left of the sternum and one on the right of the sternum! So that's what the snap, snap, snap was! No wonder I was in such pain.

My daughter was searching on the internet and found a leading Thoracic Surgeon. The head of the department at Stanford. She phoned his secretary and related my history. She also mentioned that our cousin is a doctor at Stanford.

She told the secretary, "If you don't take my mother in the next few days, it will bee too late!!" They called me back and I faxed all records to them and I was in their office within two days.

I liked Dr. Whyte, the thoracic surgeon, immediately. After going through my history, the plan was to confer with a bone specialist and a cardiologist. We had to do a needle biopsy to the sternum. The type of infection in osteomyelitis could be streptococcus, staphylococcus or a fungus. His thoughts were that I could be treated at home on an IV with antibiotics, with in-home nursing care.

On January 18th we went back to Stanford to do the pre-op directive. My cousin who is the doctor at, Stanford arrived and stayed with us the entire time. He was very supportive and explained everything to us. He knew everyone and would say "Hi" and it made me relax.

The biopsy was ultrasound-guided biopsy. They gave me a med to relax me. The last thing I remember was seeing a big needle and the doctor saying, "This isn't going to hurt, you'll only feel a little pressure." I was out!

The doctor that did the biopsy came to the recovery room to check on me. He said, "everything went well, but your doctor will probably want to do surgery to the sternum."

I thought that he just doesn't know that I'm going to be treated with antibiotics. I was kept in recovery until that night, as I didn't recover as fast as they had expected.

I went home to wait for the results. I wear glasses and would try to look down at my sternum. I could see a blue thin line. About an inch long! It had about four stitches across it. Boy! That must have been some needle. The next day I called the nurse that assisted on the biopsy. I asked her when she thought I could shower?

"Days ago"! She said.

"But you didn't put a bandage or cover of any kind on my stitches and I don't want to get them wet."

"What stitches?"

I said, "I can see them!"

She said, "You get some soap and water and wash! Those aren't stitches. Those are ball-point pen marks for guiding. And take a shower!"

She was laughing hysterically! I begged her not to tell anyone, but I know she did.

Dr. Whyte called on January 22 and said the biopsy came up with nothing. It was sterile. I had to have surgery to get a biopsy of the mass and I needed a full body bone scan. I had the scan done and picked up the written report results. But there was a mistake written about my ribs just being broken! The radiologist wrote on the report that I had hurt my ribs the previous week! I called his office and told his secretary that must be corrected before my surgery.

"It is the radiologists mistake. Dr. Whyte should be notified before surgery that the ribs broke over a year ago!"

The radiologist would not even pick up the phone. I asked the girl to look in her computer records and find when I came in for my rib injury and X-rays to verify the issue. She would not. No one in the department would help me correct the length of time the ribs were broken.

I was afraid it would be overlooked in surgery if they read it just happened. But I packed and we made the trip to Stanford.

February 1st I checked into the surgery admission unit. The nurse took me in to change and I got into my bed. They let my husband come in and stay with me. My doctor cousin arrived and he was a friend of my anesthesiologist. They began to cut up! My daughter and her fiancee were there. Everyone seemed to be having such a grand old time. They were cutting up and joking around. An IV was placed in my arm and I just drifted off.

When I came around after the operation, I was in bad shape. I hurt all over. I started drinking juice as fast as I could get it down. But I couldn't move. My chest hurt terribly. My family came in my room to cheer me up. They were wonderful. Another cousin and her husband from nearby were there. Everyone was so cheery. And then another cousin from Stanford came by. I saw more family than I had seen in a long time! This was turning out good! But it seemed to me, that my chest was very bad? Much more pain than I would have expected. This was supposed to be a biopsy?

The nursing staff kept trying to get me to sit up or move. I couldn't get my elbows under me to rise up at all. They began to threaten me to get me out of bed, but I wouldn't budge.

The head nurse was a professional clown on the side and she put her nose up to my nose and told me "Get up or get the catheter!"

Eventually I got up. She had pictures and an album of herself in clown costume. She was great! All the staff was kind and attentive. I had a hard night and would ring for morphine as soon as my time allowed.

The next morning the surgeon that assisted, stopped by to check on me. He asked if he could examine my left breast and I complied. I thought it strange, but I was tired.

89

He said I should stay another day. Of course I wanted to, since I could barely move. He asked if I had received a preliminary report. I hadn't ad he said Dr. Whyte would be in tomorrow to see me. I knew the incision in my chest was about five inches long and that the muscles were sewn together. I needed another day to make the long drive home through the mountains.

My family and other cousins came to visit. I had been in the hospital three days and was ready to leave. I got dressed and waited for Dr. Whyte. When he got there I watched his face very carefully. In the face of his assistant, I had seen the corner of his mouth do strange movements. So I watched closely. His mouth was twisting too! I got suspicious. I got scared.

He said, "we will get you the results of the biopsy as fast as we can."

I said, "What's the hurry, you're not worried are you?"

His mouth was moving! He said, "I want to move on this fast and aggressively if needed."

I started to cry and told him not to call me. I didn't want to talk to him any more! He took my hand and said he would call me and we would move fast. I didn't want to hear anymore.

My husband and I made the long drive home. When we arrived we found the new computerized kerosene monitor heater wasn't working. The house was freezing! I got in bed with an electric blanket and just shook. I thought the cold might kill me? What next? We were warm again in a few days. We have a wood stove as a back up because we lose power all the time in the storms.

My daughter came home to help care for me. We were all sitting on my big bed kidding around, when the phone call came in. It was Saturday morning and it was my surgeon.

He said, "I'm very sorry the tumor was malignant. You must go as quickly as possible to the Oncology Department at Stanford. I've already contacted the head of the department and they will take you as a patient. It was estrogen receptive and you must have cancer in your breast that had metastasized to the sternum and four ribs.

I just cried. He said I needed radiation. "Fast as we could go!"

Then he said, as plain and clear as I've ever heard a word spoken:

"I DON'T EVER WANT YOU TO EAT RED MEAT AGAIN."

The voice was big, demanding and went straight into my soul! I thought at the time, "Wow! He's Bossy!" Almost as though he was my parent. But I only thanked him for caring for me and told him "He already knew how I appreciated him".

Most of my family was right there with me on the bed and I tearfully related what Dr. Whyte said. They all consoled me and loved me throughout it. They said I would find new ways for me to eat. From this moment on, my life began to change.

At this time, on my own, I stopped taking Premarin and Provera, hormone replacement therapy. I didn't want to feed the cancer since it was estrogen and progesterone receptive. I read everything in the house on nutrition. My daughter had been a pre med student and I was loaded with books. I couldn't figure out the connection between the red meat and estrogen, but I just trusted my surgeon and went totally with it on my new diet. I figured he knew something I didn't know about food, and specifically red meat!

My husband was terrific and fed me lightly steamed vegetables and fish. I stopped using salt, sugar and meat of any kind: all fat was eliminated. All dairy was eliminated because I didn't know what was with the cows, that I shouldn't have? I thought that maybe I shouldn't have any fat? It is in red meat and perhaps that's what's wrong? I just didn't know what was with cancer and food, so I decided that anything that would stress my body had to be eliminated from my diet. Chemical and preservatives had to go.

I was healing fast by taking it very slow and easy. I had a lot of help at home and could rest. There were not any drains in my chest, so the bandages were large. My sternum got bigger and bigger and then practically exploded. We were all scared! We called the nurse at Stanford, plus a good friend and neighbor that is a nurse. Both nurses said it was normal and actually good that it happened. It was just draining, not bleeding. We live way out in the forest and you've just got to tough it out. Do the best you can. Everyone tried to keep me cheered up. No one told me at this time that they knew at the time of surgery that it was cancer. I'm glad I didn't know right away. Those few days of not knowing were used for strengthening myself.

Everyone was upbeat. Before surgery, when everyone thought it was an infection, my daughter wrote on the fridge note board, 100% recovery. She said the thoracic surgeon told her that!

"But that was for an infection!" I said.

She said, "Leave it! Never erase it! It stands!"

So no one Touches it. It's in big green letters with happy faces around. It will stay on there forever. We all stand on that statement.

(It's been 13 years now. I moved it from the front of the fridge, to the top of the kitchen cupboards. I can see it if I look way up there!)

People began to phone and drop by. I was wavering between accepting death and not even wanting to think about having a chance to live. I began to pray a lot. I would be OK and then someone would visit and say terrible, terrifying things about cancer victims and their death. I would go downhill and into a depression. It would take days to fight my way back to any semblance of mental well being. I decided to cut out of my life, and drop, anyone that upset me! Anyone, anytime! My phone calls were screened by my husband. I told anyone that got near me, in no uncertain terms, to watch what they said or I wouldn't speak to them again! It worked.

Chapter Seventeen

Living at Stanford Hospital Apartment

February 11th I went back to Stanford to have the incision checked for infection. A wick had to be put in my chest for a drain. It was terrible. The trip home was long and tiring. I shook so much from the trauma of getting into my chest again, that I took morphine. It seemed my mind couldn't take anymore trauma.

I had a small diary that I was keeping notes in. Things such as appointments. A record of everything I was eating was put into my journal. I was hungry, but I was so afraid that I might eat something wrong. I stayed on tract. I started juicing at this time. Mostly carrots and vegetables. I began vitamin therapy, but very, very low doses. I would take chlorophyll in my juice drinks. At this time I would eat vegetables for breakfast and at least three cloves of garlic a day. I ground up maitake mushrooms and took one capsule a day. So from the beginning of the diet on February 6th to the 17th all the huge veins that were visible on my legs, chest and neck shrunk to nothing! I was shocked! The pounding in my head that I had for years was gone! I was praying and praising God that I was still alive!

February 17th I called to get the appointment with Dr. Roberts, the head of Oncology at Stanford. The doctor that my surgeon had contacted. I was to be there on the 25th. So I decided to get over to Mt. Zion in San Francisco for the mammogram and ultrasound. At least that would be done while waiting for my oncology appointment. I brought all the previous 6 years of mammograms and ultrasounds with me. The tumor could be seen easily on all the tests I had in my possession. At Mt. Zion I had another mammogram and then an ultrasound. They found the lump right away in my breast.

They called it the 1 o'clock position. They wanted to do a needle biopsy, but I was too weak. My chest hurt too much to turn on my side. We made the appointment for the following week.

We arrived at Mt. Zion for the needle biopsy on Feb. 24th. Ultrasound guided was started and I was just as still as I could be. Dr. Leung was kind and tried not to hurt me. A good sample seemed impossible to obtain. For two hours the doctors tried. I was scared and it hurt as they were pushing the needle and trying so hard. I watched the ultrasound screen as the needle got into the mass. It was the same mass that had been watched for the last six years in the 1 o'clock position! The pathologist was called. He took over. Got a good sample. He put it under the microscope, turned and nodded to the other doctor.

That was too fast and I started to cry. Cat was out of the bag! They didn't know what to do. They were both so young. So they went out into the hall and talked. When they came back I told them they couldn't lie. They admitted the cells were malignant, but all reports must go through proper channels. The biopsy must be analyzed in the lab. It must be confirmed. The doctor hugged me and said breast cancer was easier to treat than other cancers. I was just getting in deeper and deeper. But now we knew this was the primary. I went home to rest and take all this in and try to understand how this could have happened. Six years of radiologist watching the mass in my breast. This journal was going to be helpful for my records.

Back to Stanford to the head of Oncology, Dr. Roberts. I took my cousin, the doctor, with me again. The resident doctor interviewed me first. The past six years of records were with me. Mammograms, ultrasounds, x-rays and bone scans were given to Dr. Chung. All the records went just down the hall and I could peek around the corner and see them going over everything. They were viewing them on the lighted walls. It took at least an hour or more. Later I would find that this practice of viewing all records, going over them carefully, was done by all the departments. This time was not to be hurried. This would be the time decisions would be made on how to proceed with your care.

Dr. Roberts came in, looked at my cousin, and said, "Do you recognize me?"

He said, "No"

"Well I tried to work for you on your research project in 1975 and you didn't hire me."

Whoops, we are off to a bad start!

Dr. Roberts said, "Perhaps it's just as well, I went on to bigger and better things."

They talked and reminisced about my cousins secretary. Everything settled down and everyone was quite amiable.

Then the attention shifted to me. Dr. Roberts excused everyone and examined me. Called everyone back in and said, "I'm going to tell you everything we know about you. You have cancer in your sternum. In two or three ribs, your breast and throughout your body. If it was not for the fact that you are estrogen positive, I would tell you there is nothing we could do for you. You will never be cured. You will never be rid of it. But we can treat you with tamoxifen. You can have a lumpectomy or a mastectomy, it doesn't matter"

I asked how long I would have to be on Tamoxifen?

He said, "I hope you can be on it for the next 20 years if you're lucky, as long as you can live."

He made an appointment for me with the breast surgeon, Dr. Jeffrey, and set up an MRI , ASAP, and set my appointment for radiation to start.

Most of that meeting didn't register in my brain. I had been warned that you must take someone with you for that kind of exam and discussion. That was the reason I took my husband and cousin, the doctor. My cousin and my husband told me details over lunch, that I couldn't remember at all! My mind just wouldn't work. I even argued over some issues with them. But they were right and I just couldn't remember. We returned home to make our next plan of battle.

On March 3rd we went back to Stanford and stayed with my cousin on campus. Back to the hospital at 5 am. It was nice to have breakfast at the hospital. Still careful even though eating out. I found ways to not deviate from my diet. My most precious thing was a good cup of coffee in the morning. I would not give this up!

The MRI took 2 hours! I was lying on my sternum and ribs! It was awful. Then to Dr. Jeffrey's office. I waited and waited for my 3 pm appointment. I was tired! But they informed me that the MRI done this morning didn't work. A Scanner malfunction. I was losing it and I had a small temper tantrum. I stomped around a bit and huffed and puffed! I was a little mean with the nurse as she got me ready for the doctor.

I finally met with Dr. Jeffrey. A very thorough and extensive exam was done. The plan is to do a lumpectomy, if in her judgment, this is still an option. Another MRI tomorrow has to be done. I'll stay another night at my cousin's.

The next day we had a successful MRI. We went home to rest and wait for our next appointment with Dr. Jeffrey.

On March 8th Surgical Specialties called to have a needle biopsy for the Sentinel Lymph node. This is a technique of finding the main node. Determining if it is cancerous and making a decision to take so many nodes at the time of breast surgery.

Off we go again at 5:30 am to Stanford. We went directly to the Radiation Department to meet with Dr. Rodgers and Dr. Bevin. I liked them both immediately. They explained all procedures of radiation treatment and all side effects. I was put on Tamoxifen that day, by that department. We went to lunch. I went to my appointment with Dr. Jeffrey and she informed me the tumor was too massive to do a lumpectomy. We must do a mastectomy. But I could consider radiation first because recuperating from another surgery would push back radiation another 5 weeks. We've got to stop the growth in the sternum, ribs and breast. I just cried and cried. A lumpectomy was out!

Dr. Jeffrey looked at me. She said, "I want you to set some long term goals, and stick to them. I want you to do all the things you've always put off doing. Do the most important things to you. Don't put it off. I will see you when I return from my vacation. Be sure to get approval from Dr. Roberts if you choose radiation first".

Stanford Hospital called on March 11th and asked me to be there in the morning to move into an apartment on the grounds. I packed the car with everything I thought I might need for the next two months and off I went. I met with everyone in radiation and paperwork was completed. All that was required to move into my apartment, completed. Fully furnished down to the linens and salt & pepper!. I could walk to my appointments and to radiation. It was very comfortable and I settled in. I bough a juicer right away. Loaded up on vegetables and cereals. Rice milk was the choice now instead of soy milk. I was still only guessing at what I was doing? I meditated and prayed a couple of times a day. I read books about people being healed all the time. I was asked to join a support group, but did not. I felt anything could undermine my determination. If I focused on the cancer instead of my body and what my body wanted, I would go backwards! Giving more power to the cancer with my attention, was a backward dangerous step.

I met with my oncologist, Dr. Roberts, on the 16 and he agreed to the plan of radiation first, then breast surgery later. I would have radiation to the sternum, breast and surrounding area. He said the cancer in the chest would always be there. He hopes radiation will stop its advance. Radiation should do the same with the breast.

I kept thinking about the statements made by the breast surgeon. I called and made an appointment after her return from vacation. When we were together I asked her what she meant by the strange statements she made.

"I want you to do things that are special to you while you still feel well."

"What does that mean?" I asked.

She said, "A person who has cancer the way you have in your ribs, sternum and breast, on the average will live about 18 months."

96

"No, it can't be!" I cried.

She said, "Yes, I stand on my earlier statement, I'm very sorry."

She called oncology and asked about stronger chemotherapy or a stronger medication than Tamoxifen. But my oncologist said no. To continue on as planned. I left, feeling numb.

It's very strange when you think you are going to die. You are afraid to hope because life seems to be out of your reach. It's too mentally draining to swing between hope and just being resigned to die. In these days and nights I began to pray more fervently. On my knees, thanking God that I was still alive. I stepped up my vegetable intake. I tried not to cry or be negative. I was juicing carrots and veggies six to eight times a day and taking supplements I had studied about.

I began to drink bottled water. At least eight glasses a day. It was very strange but I began to look better. It was very unnoticeable at first. I began to lose weight. There I was out of town with just a few clothes anyway, and the pounds were rolling off! I didn't know how much, but I knew it was a lot. My clothes were falling off!

I met everyone in the radiation department. New X-rays were taken and a CT scan. A cast was made from my waist up to the top of my back and shoulders. This was so you wouldn't move and the radiation would always hit only the spots it was meant to. I was informed that they would hit some of one lung. It couldn't be helped. More X-rays were taken when the cast was done. This time I was actually on the radiation table. It was a big half circle that could move around your body. Laser beams were crossing the room at different angles and the whole operation was computerized. It was very scary. I had five fields. The machine and the different coverings had to be changed with each field. The X-rays confirmed the accuracy of the set up and we began the following week.

There are four or five large rooms in the department. Each has a machine to radiate you. Each room has a double entry doors for protection. My radiation doctor, and Dr. Bevin told me that in 15 to 20 years my ribs might break easily. What a wonderful and exciting thought! I never dreamed anyone in the department thought I had that long. You wait a long time to see the doctors on your appointments, but it is because they confer with other doctors and go over all your records constantly. You know nothing is going to be overlooked. They always apologize for this, but I tell them not to worry.

"These moments are the most important moments of my life!" I said.

I was so thankful to be there. They are the best and I told them so.

I lived on the second floor and outside my windows was nothing but white blossoms. It was beautiful. It was like living amongst the tree blossoms! The weather was good and I would walk a lot. I would nap after radiation made me tired. Would always get at least eight hours of sleep. It was high security in the building, all computerized. You had to have codes to open the doors and garage. It was safe and I felt very secure and relaxed. I did well being alone and dealing with dying. I was at peace inside. I was resting. It was so strange?

The people upstairs were bouncing off the walls all the time and finally I had it with the noise. I ran upstairs in my robe and banged on the door. To my shock and surprise was the man with the clicker box at his waist, ticking. My husband and I had heard that ticking in cardiology, months before, and couldn't figure out the source.

I said, "I thought someone got hurt!"

He said, "I'm sorry, we'll hold it down."

He was waiting for a heart transplant. His mother was there, taking care of him. I don't know if he ever got a heart. They were there for the next two months. I figured out later that they were moving furniture each evening. A roll away bed was being shoved around. It was only a one bedroom and they were making due.

On Tuesday evenings, entertainers would come in for an hour or longer and sing or play for us. The program was arranged by Stanford. How it would lift everyone's spirit. The people in the building kept to themselves most of the time. But this was a time when everyone would be relaxed and together, if they were well enough.

I called my old boss, Mr. Paul, an attorney. The secretary is my girlfriend and we are still in Touch. I had an interview with his son, also an attorney.

I said, "I have all my records. Every mammogram, ultrasound and report shows cancer back to 1994, in the breast. I broke three ribs and cracked my sternum about a year ago because breast cancer weakened the bones. That is shown on the X-rays I have in my possession. The same two radiologist were reading all my records since 1994 and misdiagnosing me. What about all the women out there like me that think they can trust the people who are reading their mammograms? Even on TV you hear "get a mammogram every year or two, depending on our age". Well, who is training these people? I've had two different radiologists read ultrasounds wrong and mammograms too!"

"How could a brand new, young doctor, spot it in a few moments and be right! Perhaps the new school of training is better, and I should alert the world to the old schools' training!"

He said it would be a difficult if not impossible case to prove and I should have a comparative study done professionally by a team of doctors. He felt that if I only had 18 months, 17 now, and counting, it would be too hard on me to be involved in such a case.

I thanked him and visited with his secretary and another attorney, my friend of 30 years ago. We had lunch in their office. We reminisced and had a great time. I'm so fond of each of them. It was as though time stood still for a while.

I walked to the hospital each morning, weather permitting, and it was quite beautiful. The hospital was very clean. When I was here in Feb. for surgery in my sternum, I watched the girls come in to clean. They cleaned every square inch of the room, bed rails, down to the smallest detail. I told all the nurses & doctor how hard those girls cleaned. In keeping my appointments with at least 10 doctors, I got to know my way around the hospital pretty good.

Each morning I'd change into a gown in the dressing room in radiation. I was always early and would sit in the waiting room with 10 to 13 people like me, waiting for their "turn to burn". Everyone would talk openly about their case, where they were in the program and their weeks to finish. Usually it is five weeks straight and a week off to rest, then what they call the booster. The booster, as I began to observe, was a monster!!! As I saw people come to the end of their weeks and they seemed to be OK, the booster always was hard on them. Fear for the "booster" set in on me!

The lady in the next apartment was about 70 and her cancer had come back after five years of remission. It was wrapped around her spine in the back of her neck. All she had left was her booster. She had completed her five weeks many years ago. She was in a lot of pain most of the time. It was inoperable. We became great friends. We went shopping together and walked to the hospital together.

A beautiful young girl was sometimes in the waiting room but she didn't put on a gown, so I never talked to her. But the following week we kept seeing a red wagon in radiation. I stayed after my radiation that week and waited to see what was going on?

Out of one of the rooms came a little boy, about four. He was beautiful, like his mother. They put him in her arms and she looked at me.

I asked, "Is he the patient?"

"Yes, the tumor is as big as a football and they couldn't operate. The radiation takes some of the pain away for him."

I said how sorry I was and said "good-bye". I went in the dressing room and went to pieces, hidden, so no one could see me. While we all talked about our own cases to each other, in great detail, our spirits always up, even the ones that had no chance. This little boy was different to me. I could block away the others anguish and fear. I always looked for their bravery and cheer each day. The little boy, Alex, was different. It felt raw and I couldn't keep my heart from letting him into my being.

99

Every kind of cancer was in the radiation department and I'm a talker, and friendly. Some places in the head and face areas made me so frightened for them I could only fight to hide my fear. And those that had loved ones with them took them right along on the journey. Parents would cry as their children were getting radiated. I took in everything they had to tell. No one wanted a sour puss in the area! You could cry, but you had to still be upbeat! And if there was a grump, they stood out like a sore thumb! But no one would listen to me about juicing. No one would listen to me about breast cancer eating fat and growing. They wouldn't listen about meat estrogen or pesticides acting like estrogen. Everyone ate anything and everything as though there was no connection. No tomorrow. I learned more about cancer from those other patients in those six weeks, than I did from all the books. And about attitude and endurance. I just tried to be as strong as they all were. The will to live is wonderful. I grew to love some of them. Each one will be with me forever.

Even though I'm not a Catholic, I visited the Corpus Christi Monastery as often as I could at 5 pm each day. The nuns sing the vespers and it is beautiful. My oldest son Jimmy and his wife came for dinner and a visit. I took them there. The chapel is old and ornate, rich with gold and brass. The nuns would light the candles and burn incense. The large chapel was always almost empty. Their angelic voices would echo around the high ceiling. I could relax in the peaceful enchantment of it all for a few moments. It was good to be there with my son, who 35 years ago lived with me just down the street and went to nursery school a few blocks away. We all almost got the giggles because it was so quiet and intense!

I did try to find a church to go to and have someone pray over me for healing. It's been my past personal experience that all are not anointed to do this. I would interview pastors over the phone. I asked them up front if they believed they were able and anointed to do this. Some churches don't do it at all. Finally I found one and got what I thought were great directions. Off I went on Sunday morning. I got lost. As I gave up the search and started on my way back to Stanford, I spotted what I thought was the right church and went in. It was early and only one woman there. As everyone came in and welcomed me, I asked to meet pastor Robert. They said there was no pastor there by that name. Wrong church! So at this time, there was no laying on of hands and no healing service.

Chapter Eighteen

Growing Close to Other Patients

Last week, in the new cancer patient waiting area, I sat next to a young woman and her husband. The didn't speak to each other. She didn't move. Not even her feet. She had dark glasses on and I could see she had a black eye, and slightly swollen! He was dressed in western style clothes, with boots. He paced the floor in front of us. I thought to myself that I should give him a dirty look or perhaps say something. Obviously he was mean, intimidating and had hit her. I'll give him a piece of my mind! But I kept quiet.

How wrong I was! She joined us in the coming weeks for the cancer in her eye!

There were people from all over the world. Every nationality was all thrown in together. You didn't have to understand each others' language to understand the look in their eyes. Among them was a young mother from Alaska with her three children and husband. The baby was six months old. The mom's hair is starting to grow back in and she looks good. She was in an experimental program for Hodgkin's and could only get treatment if she lived at Stanford to be monitored. She was very optimistic.

The group I was scheduled with, visited and talked about our mutual problems. We would go out to lunch occasionally. Also the technicians did everything they could do, to alleviate fear. The doctors are called immediately over any issue. And they are there within a moment! I asked my doctors in Radiation Department if they had given up on me, as the breast surgeon thought the mass was very large. They both said no, "that I was fixable". That was the greatest statement!

My burns really frightened me and if the technicians spotted my fear, the doctor was called. Sometimes I felt like a big baby. But the doctors were kind and patient. You grow very fond of the people that have your life in their hands. I depended on them every day. While the fields were radiating me, I would count the seconds and pray. I count the seconds very, very slowly, so it appears that it is over before it should be. This always worked. I could control the fear this way. I would pretend it was over too soon. At this time I always remembered who helped me end up like this. I talked to some of the doctors here at Stanford about my misdiagnosis. But they can't comment on it. They would probably be sued if they said anything about misdiagnosis. I guess that's just the way it is. But a comparative study has been ordered here at Stanford. That study will confirm the tumor was the same all along at the same 1 o'clock position in the left breast since 1994.

The next step in breast cancer detection should be computer imaging, MRI and the retraining of all radiologists! Even the radiologist at the larger imaging center let the marked tumor on the ultrasound go without needle biopsy! He always said, "Don't worry, it's nothing."

I have tried to join study groups here at Stanford, especially the diet group study of 3000 women. Low fat study. I'm already well into it. But they said that because my cancer had metastasized, I couldn't be in the study. You'd think it would be just the opposite! People in radiation share what they have learned as far as aids for the body and spirit. One thing of importance was aloe vera gel. Radiation department said to put it on the burns. It helps. I bought the most potent, thick 100 % get! My fields in the sternum were dehydrating me from the burns and I couldn't swallow after each session as they burned my throat area. As the weeks progressed I got worse and worse. Radiation was burning my esophagus so I began ¼ cup of aloe vera gel with juice. It did help.

During the field on April 13th, I saw the area around the front of the breast swelling! I was very frightened and concerned. I had a meeting with Dr. Rodgers right away. I was examined and told again that we must proceed on schedule. I mentioned the 18 months that the other surgeon thought I had left to live. He said he agreed with the prognosis if I had an outbreak, for instance, in my spine.

He said, "No one can predict how this is going to go. You must meet with the breast surgeon to see if you should do the radiation booster at seven weeks in or wait until after a mastectomy?"

A meeting with my oncologist determined the decision would depend on another MRI results. It would be a mastectomy or double up on radiation. I was asked at this time to join a study of the brain and changes in hormone output under stress. I said I would.

The burns on my back, at the shoulder, were getting very bad. When I awoke in the mornings of the fifth week, I couldn't move my neck or head. The beam was going in small, but expanding as it came out my back and burned a large area. I wanted to stop because I thought I might get skin cancer. My skin was checked daily and the doctors said we must proceed. I knew that my flesh couldn't take the booster. I began to pray that the doctors would let me go home after my five to six weeks. You always get a week off before the booster.

I finished the field to my shoulder and back at five and ½ weeks. It was agreed that I could save my booster or extra two weeks for completion after breast surgery. So I was heading home soon, after two months at the apartments in Stanford.

The treatments were finally over and it was time to pack up and go home. I was pretty weak and it took me two days to carry everything out of the apartment and down to the car. All the books that people had sent to me. I had boxes of our tax files I had been working on. I had to buy a lot of casual clothes because of the weight loss. I had gone from a size 16 to a size 6. (And a 6 was baggy!) I have always been a big person. Now I'm little. Although in my mind I still feel large. I look in the mirror and I'm still big? It's strange. I understand the dynamics of women thinking they are overweight but are really thin.

Everything did fit in the car, barely! I went to the hospital for the last radiation on April 30, 1999. I said good-bye to the technicians and the doctors. I bought a thank you card for the technicians so they would place my card with all the others on those huge doors into the big machine. One of the technicians had her birthday on my same day. So I made her a doll. She loved it! I said good-bye to everyone in the department. Then made the long four-hour drive home.

After getting home, I found it would take some time before I could settle down and relax. Soak baths helped a lot with the radiation burns.

So I juice at least six to eight glasses of vegetables a day. They are usually in a carrot base. I'm taking all the vitamins that I've read about in all the alternative medicine books. Beating Cancer with nutrition, by Dr. Patrick Quillin is excellent. The Breast Cancer Prevention Diet by Bob Arnot was easy to understand and very fast reading. The underlying theme is always the same. Fresh live vegetables and fruit, organic foods only. I know that I am more severe with my diet than most of the diet programs. No sugar, no fat, no meat and dairy is more than most books recommend. I don't think I will ever be able to eat the way I used to! Especially since I learned the cancer metastasized to stage four and beyond! I continue to search around on the Internet and learn there. The new information is endless. Cancer Battle Plan, by Anne E. Frahm was a daily regime very close to mine.

A video put out by Dr. Lorraine Day is on the Internet as well as her books. She also gives out a list of all the books published on alternative medicine. My personal view is to go with the conventional medicine, as I did with the doctors at Stanford. I know they have extended my life. Saved my life, in fact. Surgery and radiation, while severe, have given me more time. Five months have passed since my surgery to the sternum. My family admitted to me that they were told when the surgeon came to the waiting room after surgery, that I had cancer. That I should be treated with radiation and chemotherapy. They never let on and pretended I was OK. I am glad that they didn't tell me the truth of the cancer right after surgery. I needed their laughter and joking at that time after surgery. I know now that they would go out in the hall and hide their tears from me. My spirit was up and happy in the hospital. I'm thankful because I needed my strength in that time frame to recuperate.

When my thoracic surgeon told me it was malignant over the telephone, I heard him say, "I don't ever want you to eat red meat again!"

I made an appointment with him to look at the incision and scar. As I was leaving I told him I was writing a book about my diet. And that I knew he saved my life by telling me:

"I DON'T EVER WANT YOU TO EAT RED MEAT AGAIN!"

He laughed!

He said "I'm a big meat eater and I would never make a statement like that!"

I said, "I've told every doctor, every department, that you never wanted me to eat red meat again!"

He said, "It was not me!"

I said to him, "Then it had to be God!"

This was the first time I knew that God had intervened and spoken to me. I realized immediately the seriousness of what was happening to me. If I lived, it was because of the diet that God set the course for.

I had gotten into some heavy discussions about meat with all the doctors at Stanford, but held my ground. I wouldn't budge on the issue. Every one felt there wasn't a connection. "Everything on the hormones in meat issue, is unproven" they would say!

On all my following visits to any doctor, any department, from that time forward, I said it was not Dr. Whyte, my surgeon, that said to "never eat red meat again".

I said it was God that spoke. And I told everyone. No one, not one doctor has ever argued with me or tried to debate with me on this issue. God spoke and I'm going to get well.

Chapter Nineteen

Living with Cancer

Another long trip back to Stanford on July 6th for a follow up with my breast surgeon. We checked in to the department and I was put in the exam room to wait for Dr. Jeffrey.

When she came in she introduced me to her new fellowship doctor that was her new assistant.

She asked, "did you get a face lift?"
"No" I said.

She came closer and asked, "Well did you have your eyes done?"

I laughed at her!

She said, "You look great, what are you doing?"

I gave her a brief overview of my food regimen. Then they began to examine me. They tried and tried but couldn't find the tumor that had been 3 cm in size. And they couldn't find the huge mass that was on the outside area of the breast.

She said, "You do not need surgery. There is nothing there."

She told the other doctor to look at my records and see her notes on the size of the tumor!

She said, "No matter what you are doing, don't change a thing!"

So I told her the other thoracic surgeon said he did not tell me to stop eating red meat.

She said, "You must have had an angel sitting on your shoulder that day. The studies on the hormones in red meat is unproven. But I want you to continue everything in the diet. The best plan is to go to Dr. Roberts in oncology on July 22nd. He will make the final decision on what to do next. Perhaps another MRI to confirm that the tumor really has shrunk or was gone completely. You do not have to return to my office again. There would be no need for that unless the tumor returned."

I thanked her and her staff. I left Stanford Hospital in a daze. I had been braced for surgery, a MRI and a sentinel node needle biopsy. Now I was being sent home. Perhaps cancer free by the same doctor that gave me just months to live.

On the long ride home, my husband, Michael, kept asking me what was wrong with me. I just felt numb. I didn't know what to think. What to believe. Is it really gone? Is it the diet? Radiation? Surgery? Would God speak to me and alter my destiny? Is it prayer and meditation? Perhaps it's everything mixed together. Is it the teas and supplements? I am almost afraid to think it could all be possible, but I don't want people to know until it's a sure thing.

But my husband has told a few people. He was so happy for me! They always ask if I am going to get off the diet and start eating everything again. Never! In the past people like me thought they were safe when a tumor had shrunk or disappeared. Then they started adding the foods and fats back into their diet that are wrong for them. The tumor starts up again and grows. The patient dies. The diet and health regimen is considered no good. It's a failure.

My diet, at this time, is just a copy of all those that have gone before me and experimented. It consists of fresh fruits and vegetables and juicing. I can have potatoes and organic bread, one slice a day. A very little pasta, depending on the ingredients: home made salsa with whole wheat tortillas and avocado is great! I have beans of all kinds and garbanzo beans: olive oil is OK, but still oil.. This is all explained in Bob Arnot's Breast Cancer Prevention Diet. No omega-6 fats. I take fish oil capsules, 10 grams a day. Indole-3 carbinol is an estrogen blocker.

July 22 I had to go back to Stanford Hospital for oncology appointment. I went to the breast surgeon's secretary first and asked if a copy of the final report could be mailed to me. Then I went to radiation and asked for a final report from them also, to be mailed to me. Then to oncology to see if I could get in early? They were packed, so I sat all day waiting for my appointment. There is always so many patients waiting. They are at all different phases of cancer staging. Some are so thin and frail. The chemotherapy can devastate the body. If someone is really bad, I try not to look directly at them. I feel too guilty for looking so healthy. Even though I am going through the same fear, I feel guilt. It's very strange. It's so primitive. I would take the chemo in a minute, if it came down to the line. Just for the chance to live, no matter how devastating. My cancer has really gone too far for me to ever fight a decision about chemotherapy. So I sat there for four hours. I couldn't get in sooner.

Finally I was brought into the exam room. I updated Dr. Chung, who is the "fellow" for Dr. Roberts, about being dismissed by the breast surgeon because she couldn't find the tumor. I told her of my no salt, no sugar, no fat, no dairy and no meat diet. She wrote everything down and left to get the head of oncology to examine me. Dr. Roberts came in and took my hands and turned them over, palms up!

He asked "How many carrots do you eat a day?"

I said, "Four glasses mixed with apples. Sometimes with celery and other vegetables."

I also informed him that the breast surgeon told me, "I don't care what you are doing, or what you are taking, just keep it up. Do not change a thing".

She can't find the tumor, I said.

He didn't seem very pleased! In fact, he was annoyed! He left for a phone call and came back with the head of radiation! My doctor, Dr. Rodgers! They acted angry at me! They tried and tried to find the tumor, but couldn't.

He said, "You've got to get back into radiation!"

"No!" I said, "I need a MRI to confirm any shrinkage or changes. I will have breast surgery, if needed and then perhaps more radiation."

They acted as though I wasn't there and said between themselves, "If we give her a mastectomy will she still need radiation? Yes! Lets re-calibrate her with a cat-scan and giver her 3 more weeks of radiation."

"No, I want a MRI first, as a comparative study with the previous 2 MRI's. Then my breast surgeon will decide on a mastectomy or a lumpectomy."

They said, "The surgeon can't operate if there isn't a lump."

Then my oncologist said, "The breast surgeon knows that you can never be cured and she just doesn't want to put you through anything more. She doesn't want to do surgery on you."

I said, "No, she wouldn't do that."

"Yes" he said, "The cancer is all over you!"

I felt so confused as to what to agree to next? I was slipping and going to break down and cry! But I held my ground! I wouldn't cry in front of them. It's my life and I am in this body. I call the shots! I knew I had been right about a lot of timing in this course of medical care and decision making.

And so I said, "No" to more radiation and insisted on an MRI. They finally agreed. I said I would contact them after a decision was made. It was evening by the time I left Stanford. I didn't go home. I drove on to Santa Cruz to my daughter's. I cried and cried off and on for a few days. But she got me back on track and said not to be such a wimp!

Two days later I made the long drive home.

On July 26th Michael and I were back at Stanford for another MRI. I am a terrible claustrophobic and all my MRI's had been in an "open" machine. But the radiologist, Dr. Daniel, came up to me and asked if I could possibly do the regular MRI? I started to cry.

He said, "The image is better. I would sedate you and streamline the contrast time. We'll go as quickly as we can."

They let me look at the machine and I said I would try. But they had to have someone hold my hand. The nurses and technicians took turns. I did it! The images were viewed and were complete. I was released and we went home.

Waiting for the results seemed like an eternity. Early Thursday, July 29th , a call came from a very soft-spoken man. The doctor calling was a colleague of my breast surgeon. He explained that she had gone to Scandinavia for five weeks of lecturing. But she had reviewed the MRI results and read the comparative study in the computer before she left. She had conferred with him with instructions to give me her prognosis. He said the tumor had shrunk by one third and that it could be dead. He told me these were very positive results and that I had three choices. I could come back to Stanford now and have a needle biopsy. I could wait five to six months to see if there was more shrinkage and have another MRI study. Or, when my breast surgeon returned, I could have a lumpectomy and a biopsy.

I said I would be happy to wait for my surgeon. I would set up the appointment for a lumpectomy.

No words can describe how proud I was of my doctor. Only 48 hours have elapsed since the MRI and she got the results before they were even out of the computer. I know how pressed she was for time. Particularly before a trip of that length, but she had remembered! She cared and she saved me a lot of anguish by being thorough. She has always given me the freedom of different choices. She put a lot of decision making in my hands. It kept me strong and fighting. "Keep up whatever is working, don't change a thing!" she would say.

After another five weeks, around September 5th, I got a call to come back to Stanford for an open MRI. When the two tumors were found, a wire would be placed around them. I was scheduled for an open MRI guided core biopsy. I thought it was going to be a piece of cake, so I went alone to Stanford and planned to travel on to Santa Cruz after wards.

I was early. Contrast dye was placed in my arm and I was placed into the big halo MRI on my stomach. There is an opening in the halo mid-way. A big tray was brought in and I was numbed in the area. A sample was taken with a large needle, and another and another. There was terrible pressure and a lot of pain.

"How many more?" I asked.

"Just a few more," he replied, "you have three sites that are suspicious and one we have to go through your breast to get to."

Oh no, maybe I chose the harder way to go! There were fifteen biopsies in all. I was so thankful when it was over.

"That was harder than surgery would have been on you", he said. "You must understand that this is not a guarantee that there is no cancer. I did my very best. It is 95% accurate and we will have the test results in a few days. You must return in a year for an open MRI comparative study to check the size of the tumor." Ice packs were placed around the breast and I was on my way to Santa Cruz. I was so thankful it was over.

The test results showed proliferative fibro-cystic change including stromal fibrosis and ductal hyperplasia. Results were consistent with irradiated breast tissue. There was no evidence of carcinoma in all 15 samples! What a joy. All the samples were written up as a yellow-tan color? Could that be the carrot juice? I didn't ask. I was just too happy. It didn't matter anyway, because no one would believe me.

Chapter Twenty

Trying to Eat Only Fruits & Veggies

Almost a year has passed now, since I learned on February 6th 1999 that I have stage four cancer, and that I might not live. I have lost a few friends to cancer and some acquaintances. I've tried to give out the diet. It's rarely taken very seriously. But a friend is on it and doing very well. I hear of people that know of others that are doing it and have success. I feel and look pretty good. Although my sternum aches and I can't turn onto my side at night in bed. The CT and bone scans show the hole is still here in my sternum. The breast cancer ate the bone marrow in my sternum. My skin is still dark and burned. The ribs that broke as the cancer ate through them, still hurt. I am afraid anytime there is pain in that area. Afraid that it is active and on the move. It takes a good deal of effort to trust fruits and vegetables! And not the symptoms! The Tamoxifen causes ongoing hot flashes. It's hard to sleep. I am dehydrated from the radiation and need water all through the night. My mouth is parched when I wake up in the middle of the night and need liquid, fast. I believe all this is just par for the course with the after effects of radiation and Tamoxifen. So this seems small potatoes in exchange for being alive!

I have some special foods that are like deserts and treats for me. Toast with a bit of almond butter and sugarless fruit is wonderful with a cup of tea or coffee. Salsa and organic chips that do not have any salt. I appreciate the food I eat and am very aware now of how I feel if I get any chemicals by accident. I seem to be intolerant now to anything that is not good for me. I have flax oil for butter and squish avocado with it on toast! I only use flax oil now on my salads, unless I make the salad dressing myself.

I am very uneasy as there are only six days to go until the year is up for knowledge of wrongdoing.

Since I seem to be doing so well I've decided to go to a new oncologist, closer to my home. All my records have been transferred to him. He is very thorough and said 1 in 20 can survive. I told him that was good enough for me. I told him God spoke to me and that I would live. He smiled and didn't argue with me. No one argues with me.

But the constant care and vigil of a case, such as mine, is all time consuming! CT scans and bone scans are every 3 months for CT and 6 month intervals for bone scan. I have terrible claustrophobic attacks and have threatened to tear the machines apart if they didn't get me out! They hate to see me coming! But I will say, most technicians know how to talk me down and get me into the machines.

I have had many mistakes made just in the wording on the CT reports. "Increased" uptake words would send me into a tail spin! Although treatment will not "cure" bone metastases, there can be remission. A change of any kind would mean more test and a change in medication. I went from being confident to being scared to death at the change in just a word or two!

So I'm still on course. The voice of God that said, "I DON'T EVER WANT YOU TO EAT RED MEAT AGAIN!" Made all the difference in my life and I follow it like a commandment.

If I live, my story will continue. I have devoted this last year to fighting for my life in relation to understanding what's going on inside my body. I have a strange confidence. I heard God speak! To think I could live awhile longer. It's wonderful. No one can take that away from me. The doctors are kind to me when I remind them of God's statement. They always smile. Perhaps God knew in advance that I would be curious and read about the issue of red meat.

I wrote another book on the spread of Bovine Spongiform Encephalopathy (BSE) disease in cattle feed that includes the rendered remains of animals carrying an infectious prion protein known to cause spongiform. Prions survive incineration at 360 degrees for one hour, irradiation, autoclaving (sterilizing under high heat and pressure), burial in the earth for at least three years and so on. Mad cow disease. But that's another story.

A call from my oncologist just came in on the results of the last CT scan. He said he could see the area that had the radiation in the sternum, the surgery area and the hole is still there.

He said, "It's not pretty! But nothing has changed in six months, since the last CT. That's great. It couldn't be better!"

So just a year ago I walked through those big doors at Stanford. Scared, lost and not knowing my way around. More than 13 doctors and countless others that I never met personally, worked together, to perfection. Different departments communicating and directing my care, smooth and precise. I will be eternally grateful and thankful to them and to God for each day they have given me. No matter how long.

Chapter Twenty-One

Cancer Returned

After a year passed I did begin to relax a little on what I would eat. Still not any red meat, but some butter on baked potatoes, breads and sweets. I gained about 15 pounds and felt that the affects of Tamoxifen had failed. They expected only a year of suppression of the tumors. So I was put on Arimadex. Since the cancer was all over me they did not want me to suffer needlessly. A mammogram showed the tumor growing faster and larger. I decided to have a mastectomy. It was hard on me because within two weeks I was hospitalized for appendicitis. Then a mass showed on my pericardium. The doctors at Stanford felt I might have a chance with chemotherapy.

I started a very hard regime called CAF, Cytoxan, Adriomyacin and F5 floriconal. Very very hard chemo. Within three weeks I was hospitalized for neutropenia and infection. I got another oncologist, closer to home and my doses were lowered just a fraction. But I could tolerate it.

Toward the beginning of March 2002, I wanted to stop the chemo. I'd had enough and the tumor was not shrinking at all. I had CT's every 30 days and no change. I had almost finished the full course of chemotherapy and had to go back to Stanford for a checkup. I had a CT done to take with me to Stanford, the day before. It showed the tumor was still the same size , at 4 cm x 2 cm.

I packed and knew I would stay for a day or two at Stanford. While driving this Sunday morning, there was time to kill, as my appointment was for Monday morning. I pulled off the freeway and drove to a church I knew. It was the same large church that

115

I had visited and the old Prophet called me out. I spoke of it earlier in this book. As I went in, and was greeted, I asked the pastor if they had a healing service.

"Yes. You can come forward after the service and ask the elders to pray over you" he said very quickly and almost abruptly!

Well the service was nice and a lot of beautiful singing. I was dressed up and had a little matching hat on. No one could see my bald head. When the service was over, I went forward, with many, many people. Lots of elders were praying over people and I was very moved by it. But as I leaned forward with my head down and was crying a little bit, my hat fell off!

I didn't know what to do and it made me cry in frustration! But the pastor saw! He saw my bald head! And he came charging over to me! He was shouting my healing! Yelling over me! In my ear! Demanding the cancer leave! "In the name of Jesus" he would call out! Over and over he commanded the cancer to leave me!

I was just weak and limp. I stayed with my head down and finally after most people were gone, I put my little hat back on. Got back on the freeway and drove on to Stanford.

The next morning I had to have another CT at Stanford. It was explained that it was needed for comparisons in the future, at Stanford only. So I said OK.

I stayed another night and went on to my appointment in oncology in the morning. The CT's were all there for comparison. The nurse came in and started the exam. Then the oncologist came in.

"The tumor is gone" he said.

"No! That's impossible. I have been on chemo for almost six months and had CT's all the time. The tumor would not shrink on the chemo! I had a CT three days ago and the tumor was there!"

"Well it's gone now. The chemo must have worked" he said.

I thanked him and left.

I knew what had happened. The chemo could not get that tumor down, but God could and did! When the pastor prayed over me, he had the power. He had the Anointing to demand that the cancer leave me. His name is Pastor Roger Houtsma and I am still in Touch with him.

As I write now and complete this book, over ten years have passed. I have never eaten red meat again. I will never eat red meat again. I still try to be careful what I eat and juice.

I am thankful each moment.

I researched on line and found a chemo drug that was being used in Europe. At this time, in 2003, it was not available or legal in the U.S.

It was an aromatose inhibitor called Faslodex. I pleaded with my new oncologist to let me try it. He contacted Astrazeneka. They agreed to a trial, compassionate study. And there was no cost to me at this time. An injection once every 28 days. I responded to it very well and have now been on it for over 9 1/2 years. I am the longest living survivor on this drug.

As I gained my strength back I chose to have my remaining breast reduced to very, very tiny as a precaution.

It was a very good choice.

As my health returned, I started a very unique on line business. It was a very successful endeavor, overnight. But a lot of paperwork and record keeping. All the tax and legal issues were trying and time consuming. Any writing was put aside and almost forgotten.

Occasionally someone would ask to take a look at their Aura. Or one of our kids would bring someone over to check their body, stomach or whatever. As my husband was still so reluctant to look at people or "Touch" their head, he would rarely see anyone.

At this time we only knew that my husband could close his eyes and see into your complete body. Inside everything and outside aura and halo. This includes illness, infection, anger, stress, worry, broken bones, surgeries or anything. Everything is seen in colors and then gray and dark or light. Wellness or illness, love or hate, it can all be seen. Anger is the most damaging thing we have ever seen. A black energy that won't subside until anger is released and leaves the mind and body in forgiveness or understanding. I had a big, big temper long, long ago and we watched black move in my upper torso if I threw a temper fit!.

If he "touched" a person with his right hand on the forehead, most times, past lives would be seen. Sometimes this life, with the person as a child. Each person looks very much like themselves, recognizable. The clothes and surroundings give a glimpse of the time period.

Most people were fascinated with their past life. But it is only a glimpse of them. There is never revealed anything that is too personal or invasive. It is a very gentle unfolding. As if the person already knows intuitively, their past, their injuries and what they are working out.

117

One very interesting couple came to visit from the Ukraine. They were in their late fifties. A "Touch" with the right hand to the forehead revealed the wife in a great open grassland. Dancing in an ethnic yellow, red, and very detailed costume. Perhaps over 100 years or so ago. Celebrating with a very large group and dancing and celebrating. Long long ago as wagons and the village could be seen.

Then with his right hand, Michael "touched" the forehead of the husband. He was in the same costume! But with pants or short pants on? In the same open grasslands. So it means they knew each other, then and now. We have recorded this happening, often. People meeting each other, again and again.

Then one day I asked Michael to "Touch" my forehead with his right hand and left hand on the back of my head. He saw the inside of my head! We were surprised! Sometimes it looked like steel wool and the center of my head would have a light spot. Sometimes nothing but the steel wool wire type of lines. The background of the lines is a soft rose color. Sometimes the center is dark or light? The center can change but the lines are always seen.

We were just relaxing on the couch one afternoon. My head hurt and I am often worried that the cancer might return. Stanford kept warning me that stage four breast cancer can go to the brain. So this particular day, I was tired. I leaned over and rested my head on his chest.

I asked, "Would you look at my head carefully? Inside my brain? See if there are any dark spots? I don't feel good and my head hurts".

So Michael put his right hand on my forehead and the left hand on the back of my head. But I was so tired and weak that I leaned in closer to him and rested my head, my right temple, on his forehead.

So my right temple was resting on his forehead.

Michael said, "Don't move! I can see things that I have never seen before!"

So this was something new to us. It was not the same as seeing what we assumed was past lives. What Michael was now seeing was not me. So began the record of something new. Every few days we would look in the new "Touch" with two hands and to the forehead. There were different visions of scenes above the Earth! The whole Earth. Great expanses of sea and clouds. Some visions had deep spiritual meaning or thought provoking ideas. More and more often Christ Jesus was appearing. But we didn't know what to make of it all?

I stepped up my meditation time to 1/2 hour two or three times a day. I searched scripture and studied more and more. My prayer time on my knees was hopefully twice a day for 15 minutes.

I tried to log most of what Michael would tell me he saw. I've kept notes and drawings and pictures of things that were similar to what he was seeing. Everything changes so quickly and then is gone. And we forget quickly if I don't write it down right away! I write as fast as I can, on any scrap of paper that is handy. I've tried to date everything, but notes get lost and then out of order and then found. So sometimes things are repeated. This book might seem jumbled because it is put together from notes!

I closed down my business to stop everything but this book. The notes began to come together and the logs grew and grew. The next few years were spent in searching in meditation and prayer. As well as all the information I could find on the healing of the wounded child. There is a world of information on healing on the internet.

So, with the right hand and the left hand on my head, the "Touch" took on an unfolding of its own. We have tried to record everything Michael saw. Some notes are still being found that are only meaningful to me or too personal to have meaning in this book for anyone else.

Michael and I try not to draw any conclusions when we do not understand what the "Touch" reveals. We have made many mistakes in interpretation. So for years we just kept looking inside my head and keeping notes.

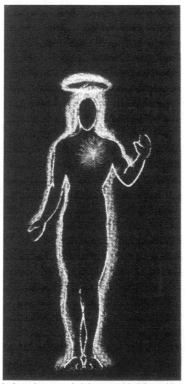

Love of humans causes halo to be seen brighter and brighter. Heart center glows with love.

119

Chapter Twenty-Two

Revealing of Letters and Words

September 19, 2010: This morning I tried again, to pray. On my knees, with my hands open in front of me. My arms are extended a bit forward. After five to ten minutes of praising God, I can feel the falling of the Glory Light. With my eyes closed, I can feel the energy in my bones, chest, face and head and heart area. After a time, I asked my husband to look at me.

The light all around me was huge and golden. My whole chest area was white and glowing. I could feel it. A radiating warm energy.

October 10, 2010 I have continued to pray in this manner. Always, only praising God. Simply put, this is a time of worship. To use this time to direct my praise to Jesus, Lamb of God, who overcame death. To Jehovah, "Hallelujah". Praying on my knees, with arms forward and palms open. During this period of time, the power falls on me after five to six minutes. Sometimes it is so strong my bones in my face hurt, or I fall over and am unable to breathe for a time. Perhaps there is something in me that needs to be cleared up?

October 15, 2010 "Touch" revealed a huge hour glass over the earth. The sands of time were running out. It was in clouds above the earth. Next came a dark robed figure standing in swirling clouds on top of the earth. The cloaked figure was a skeleton or death figure, in a dark hooded garment. His two arms held a huge sickle and it was raised

121

and ready to swing toward the earth. As if to reap?. I do not know if this is imminent? We could not interpret or explain the meaning of this.

October 22, 2010 "Touch" revealed a great swirling, violent sea (ocean) turbulent! But near the shore was a rock! A rock so massive that it was unmoved by the turbulence of the crashing sea. The rock was unmovable. Then a rolling mountain range appeared. Not too high or steep. Many people, a multitude of people, were on top of this low mountain. They were gathered with hands raised, praying and praising God. My interpretation is: turbulence is near. The rock is to stand firm. Stand firm. Solid as a rock! Then climb higher in the Spirit. It is not a steep climb. The mountain is not that high to climb. Above, you can praise and pray in the Spirit!

October 23, 2010 "Touch" revealed a dome. Not a glass dome. But covering praying. An energy covering or hindering praying. Next revealing that the pouring out on me was never filling up! Like pouring out into a glass, but never filling up! Never more than half full. A leak! Still must be something wrong with me.

In The evening the "Touch" revealed a girl caught in a web. Trying and trying to break free.

I asked the Lord, silently, to myself, "please, tell me what to do and show me how to learn what to do next"? My husband touched me and saw:

Jesus, lighting a flame, (a candle or lamp) and leading me. Beckoning me to follow Him! That makes me happy! So simple.

November 4, 2010 The "Touch" revealed a dove watching me on my knees, in prayer and praise. My hands were lifted and palms open, just in front of me.

November 5, 2010 I'm very tired and did not sleep very well, last night. After praying and praise the Glory light was surrounding me and my halo was very, very light. I am listening to a healing CD . Pressing in and praying.

November 6, 2010 My husband looked at me and saw that I was very dark. My head and halo and body were dark when I woke up. The "Touch" revealed that I was on a treadmill? Showed that I should have been under an apple tree having a picnic! To get rid of that, I went into prayer and praise! Within 15 minutes, light surrounded me and my halo was white! I'm pressing in!

This evening, I asked my husband to pray for me about why such a struggle when

I sleep? The "Touch" revealed that I should pray and meditate before falling asleep. Otherwise, as I fall asleep in peace, a great storm and darkness are coming. The Holy Spirit, as a huge dove, has to fight the turbulent storm for me! Holding back the storm, away from me, with wings as big as the storm! I will wait on the meaning of that.

November 23, 2010 After praying, the "Touch" revealed the Glory light falling on people praying on their knees. The praising and praying on the knees showed many receiving or it can be only one receiving. The light fell on one or many as their hands were raised.

November 26, 2010 After prayer and praise time I could feel the warmth in my chest area. The "Touch" revealed there was a large flame, yellow and red and gold, small at the bottom and large and flaming at the top. I drew a picture of it and my husband confirmed that it was accurate.

In the evening, after praying, it was brought to my attention, very gently, that a wound or a childhood trauma is brought to the surface by a similar attack. A verbal attack can bring up 5 year old child's attack. A five year old's feelings. Similar feelings and similar reaction. Pain and threat of loss of loved ones.

December 15, 2010 "Touch" revealed the 'Lamb of God' in the center of the "Flame". Pure praise, uncomplicated and simplified praise, makes the powerful connection to the Holy Spirit. Wow!! The "Touch" revealed the Dove hovering. I asked "What is it? What is this power that falls on me?" The answer shown to us is the "Dove, The Holy Spirit"—It is all making perfect sense now. I am so thankful. Thank you Lord Jesus for being the Lamb of God! My tears are of joyful thankfulness.

JANUARY 1, 2011 I am very tired and low in spirit. "Touch" revealed a little, small frail donkey. It has a huge load strapped on its back. It is climbing up a steep, steep, mountain trail. —my interpretation is,— I am carrying too big a load.

January 2, 2011 "Touch" revealed the little donkey, walking, stopping, and walking and stopping again. Then the donkey was trying to climb up a small hill with the oversized load! Took a few steps and stopped. Only to try again. Behind the small hill is a valley beyond. Then flat land with a huge mountain in the distance—interpretation is, another mountain to climb. A lesson to experience, just pass the valley.

January 3, 2011 This morning we discussed how hard it is for me to let God do the work. I'm sure I will learn.

January 5, 2011 Mourning "Touch" revealed the little donkey stopped to drink water. This means resting, refreshing and not climbing.

Afternoon "Touch" revealed Christ praying near a large rock.

Evening "Touch" revealed Christ coming down the mountain trail. His arms were open as He walked, slowly, slowly down.

"Touch" revealed a white horse standing next to the little donkey. The donkey is so small and still heavy laden with the strapped on packs! It is next to the larger, beautiful white horse.

Late evening, the "Touch" revealed the white horse is next to little donkey. Still heavy laden with strapped packs. Both are now looking up, to the hill above. The Lord is walking down the hill, carrying a staff. Behind Him there is a large flock of sheep. They are spread out all over the hill, following the Lord, downward on the soft slope of the hill. The donkey, heavy laden, and the white horse, just continued to look upward to the Lord coming down the trail.

January 6, 2011 Morning "Touch" revealed the little donkey, alone, but still heavy laden. Stopped and looking back. The mountain ahead was covered on top with a billowing, swirling clouds. Churning and tumultuous. The little donkey did not step. It just looked back, and side to side.

January 7, 2011 "Touch" revealed the little donkey, stopped, looking side to side. The path up the mountain is smooth and clear. But both sides of the path have huge boulders on either side. Donkey won't take a step!

January 8, 2011 Morning prayer. "Touch" revealed the little donkey passed through a large canyon, on the path, with huge boulders on each side. The path is steep, up to a mountain, just ahead. The path is again, clear, but straight upwards. Up the mountain path, and as always, shown, huge boulders on both sides. I take this to mean that the path has been traveled and laid out before me.

I asked, "Look to the top of the mountain"! See what you can see".

There was the Lord. He was in front of what appeared to be the disciples. They were on their knees, praying. They were bathed in a bright light! They were shinning, and the light was coming, emanating from the Lord. As though He was blessing them. Their heads were down.

January 13, 2011 "Touch" revealed the little donkey kicking back legs and bucking! A good fight sign. Evening "Touch" revealed Christ seen on a hill top. Rolling hills and a staff in His hand. Thousands and thousands of sheep are all around the top of the rolling mountains, around Him. At dusk or dawn, we couldn't tell.

January 14, 2011 Evening "Touch" revealed the little donkey, still carrying the heavy load. Stopped.. Looking over side of mountain, to the trail below. Deep valley below, with the trail far, far below. Donkey has come a long, long way.

January 29, 2011 Saturday morning. Struggling for many days now. Seems time is just racing by! With company, guests overnight and family, the minutes slip into hours and it seems there is no time to write. But this morning "Touch" revealed letters. Moving letters that were going by too fast to read or understand. This was the first time that Michael saw the letters clearly displayed!

January 30, 2011 Sunday morning prayer time was spent praising on knees, hands open for around ten minutes. Then praising prayer out loud another ten minutes. Then quiet in meditative silence, thanksgiving only in silence for five minutes. The outpouring was very powerful! Especially in the center of my chest area and heart. Also in the throat area, a warm and loving energy. Peaceful outpouring from God. The most powerful yet.

The "Touch" revealed me praying and meditative silent praise. The question was, "is this position and speaking aloud and then silent correct"?.

I had a huge white, golden glory light on my chest. It was square like a shield! Up to my chin. Huge white glow around me, like an aura and Big, big halo!

February 9, 2011 "Touch" revealed the little donkey climbing, but pulling, only a tiny, tiny little cart on the trail, up the mountain! Heavy load is getting smaller! I'm learning!

February 10, 2011 "Touch" revealed a "head" or skull enclosed in glass or some kind of enclosure?? The way of release is shown "Moses parting the Red Sea". His arm was raised with the staff in his hand.

So the interpretation is, parting the Red Sea and crossing over to the other side. Go into the promised Land. Go into the fullness of the Spirit! Jesus referred to Moses lifting up the staff, as he would be lifted up.

February 11, 2011 My help has been daily prayer, study and uncovering the truth of my wounds. To do this task, of working on just one wound, has taken weeks. The tapes, CD's, and books, that have helped me understand the dynamics of wounded children, and the consequences are: Paul Hegstrom's CD's, Katie Sousa's CD's, Caroline Myss, and James Finley's "Transforming Trauma" and Sid Roth's "Supernatural Healing" book. God has been my guide and I am now open to do whatever it takes to be totally free from any limitation that the wounds put on me.

Because of all the teaching and feeling that I understood, I wanted to try or attempt just one wound. So on Feb 11th I called my sister and asked for the phone number of my brother. As I dialed the number great waves of panic and fear and unrest came over me. But I knew he was blind in one eye, broken, and weak. Compassion and forgiveness became stronger than the fear and unrest. I chose to forgive. I chose to try to help him in some small way. I talked to a sweet nurses aid and she advised me to call back in a day to find if he needed anything. When I hung up the phone, for the first time in 67 years, there was nothing but kindness toward him. I knew there was no hold on me. If I had not been observing myself and watching what forgiveness would do, I might not have felt it all. It was so subtle and in my spirit! But so powerful! I was free of this particular wound. By my choice to forgive, God does the rest. I vowed to always cherish this state of forgiveness. It has worked.

February 15, 2011 Because I am not a writer, I am just going to tell the truth. Not watered down. Not edited. Just written quickly and tell what "the Touch" reveals. We asked the Lord to reveal if this is how and what I am to write? The "Touch" revealed a straight flying arrow!! I am on track! Straight arrow! I am excited.

February 18, 2011 Morning "Touch" revealed me being tossed in a blanket. Thrown way up high. Again and again. I do not know the meaning?

February 22, 2011 The "Touch" after prayer in the morning revealed a shape like a tear drop. A huge teardrop shape. Approximately eight feet tall, over me. Then it changed to the same shape, aglow, over people. It was aglow and lighting over them.

March 4, 2011 This morning "Touch" revealed Jesus ministering to a small group of people on their knees. His arm raised, holding a staff, but a crucifix was on the top of the staff! He was showing it to kneeling people.

I had to wait and study for the meaning of this revealing. It means to look to the crucifixion, as the means of freedom. To receive the free gift! Healing power and freedom. The gift is lifted to see! To accept! Miracle demonstration of Divine power and authority! The breaking of all curses!

In the hands of Commanders and prophets, the walking stick was called a staff. In the hands of rulers and kings, the staff was called a scepter. Their staffs or scepters symbolized power. Very very important revealing!

March 4, 2011 Afternoon "Touch" revealed men in white cloaks or robes. They had a large red cross on their chest area. One held up a large goblet. But the goblet became brighter and brighter! Glowing golden and white. It was too bright for them and they covered their faces and eyes. They turned away from the intensity of the brightness! Then Christ appeared and they turned back, to look at him.

March 7, 2011 After morning prayer the "Touch" revealed the Lord standing in a long white robe. He had a long red collar. Very long and very wide on top of the white robe. He was standing in front of me. I was praying. His hands were on each side of my head. Then above some tree tops, a Dove, the Holy Spirit flew high above the tree tops. Then the Dove dropped below and out of sight. I would not try to interpret this.

March 11, 2011 Spent the day with my grand daughter's birthday party. Chasing kids and having a grand time! Evening spent watching the news and inter-net news of the Japan tragedy.

In the early evening I started getting a strange trembling all over my body. Especially in the chest area! I could not stop shaking. I asked my husband to look at me. In the area of my chest, where the square of light usually is, there was a huge lion head. Bigger than my whole upper torso. Just the head. A male lion. Big mane and wider than my shoulders. I said I did not know what that meant??

So I got on line and searched.

It was the Lion of Judah. It is YESHUA! The Lion of Judah. The "Touch" revealed The Lion and then the morning sun coming up. I do not know what it all means?

Later in the evening, at bedtime, I felt the trembling again. I asked my husband to look at me and sure enough, the Lion was at my chest area again. Covering the front of me from the waist up to my chin. I still don't know what it means???

March 13, 2011 This morning "Touch" revealed the Lion again. But a violent wind was behind Him! All His mane was flying forward around His head! Swirling and making a shadow around His eyes. A great wind!???? Then a scene from Japan appeared. The water rushing in. Perhaps something else is coming?????

Then it disappeared from view and a high post appeared. Just a post. But it began to turn and it showed to be the cross. It moved out of view and a dove appeared. Flying high in light and then flying out of view.

March 14, 2011 "Touch" revealed a great wide ocean. As far as the eye can see. Perhaps the Pacific Ocean, as we live next to it. Then very high up in the clouds, on the clouds, was the Lord. Standing and a great light was around Him and a circle of Light around His Head.

I asked what should I do? The revealing was me, praying on my knees. I had my left hand on a book and my right hand was raised and open and in a praise position!

March 15, 2011 The "Touch" revealed the white horse. Running in front of a great storm. There was lightening and swirling storm behind him. He was out running the storm! I don't know what the white horse is?

After prayer and praise time, this morning, the white horse is running and far behind him are a few other horses. Dark horses, but the white horse outruns them. Swirling sand or dirt being churned up behind the horses. Running toward the left, as facing me. I told my husband that I don't know how to interpret this. Try again. The next "Touch" revealed the white horse close, very close and big. Alone and going in the opposite direction?

This evening the "Touch" revealed the white horse running or trotting along side of the Lion! They just move along together, side by side? They did stop and looked side to side and rested.

March 16, 2011 "Touch" revealed the white horse and The Lion are very close. The white horse shook his mane and head. Very beautiful and large. Very up close. In your face. I asked, who or what are they? And is the white horse the Holy Spirit. Everything vanished and a flying dove appeared.

This second vision, "Touch", is completely different from the Lion and White Horse subject. Because the Knights Templar have appeared many times before.

I just did not know of the connection.

I asked again. Where is the rider or is there a rider of the white horse?

A large shield appeared with a red cross on it. It was down to the lower leg of a rider. Then a view from above, that the rider had Armour. His armour was as silver. The shield was silver. Large silver helmet with slits at the eyes. I do not know or attempt to interpret this?

After much research, I found it was a Knights Templar. I have started a study of them and the Kabbalah. The Knights Templar acquired the Jewish Temple of treasure and Mystical Jewish Cabalah knowledge. I don't know what this means?

March 20, 2011 The morning "Touch" revealed an old, old man leaning over a large box. He was just looking inside. There was light glowing up and out of the depth of the box. I don't know or attempt to interpret this?

The morning "Touch" revealed The Holy Spirit as a Dove flying over an empty nest. Shining light over the empty nest.

March 24, 2011 This morning "Touch" revealed a stack of gold. A huge pile of gold, shining!?

March 25, 2011 Morning "Touch" revealed ancient Jews with head coverings, like a turban. They were standing in a circle. Perhaps twenty or thirty? Looking into a large stone edged well. They were far out in a desert place. They began pushing and shoving each other as they each tried to get closer to the deep, dry well or hole? There was no water showing, but a golden light coming up from the bottom! It got brighter and brighter!

I can not begin to interpret this, at this time?

This afternoon I began to get chest pains. If I laid flat and did not move, they would go away. We live so far out in the woods, that I did not want to make anything out of it. But just lay still. I could not walk at all. But during the evening, my family convinced me to go to the emergency room. The pain persisted, even at the hospital. A CT and EKG showed nothing, all normal. Went home and rested and slept.

March 26, 2011 I just stayed in bed and did not move. Pain in chest in the radiated area, of eleven years ago, persisted.

March 29, 2011 The morning "Touch" again revealed the dark cloaked, hooded being (Seen with the October 15, 2010 "Touch" page 121.) high above the earth on swirling clouds. The same figure as before, with the sickle! But this time the sickle was swirling above his head. Around and around! I don't like this. I don't even want to know what it means. But I will just keep writing what is shown to me.

I asked On February 20 2013 "Is the reaper swirling his sickle during the great tribulation?" Michael touched my head and the "Touch" revealed:

"AFTER"

March 31, 2011 This morning "Touch" revealed a huge whale, dead on the beach. It could mean more problems with Fukushima?

Then it changed to the sky. Brilliant and colorful with the center as a huge white sun or golden hole? Swirling white clouds and colors all around it! The Heavens opened!

"Just beautiful", my husband said. And running on through, the expanse of the earth, was the white horse. Running across the green grass.

I don't know what it means? But might interpret later today.

April 2, 2011 In the evening, the "Touch" revealed the Lion. All alone and up very close, looking into our eyes! I don't know what this means.

April 3, 2011 The huge Lion is resting. Just sitting and looking.

April 4, 2011 This morning I asked the Lord, "the problem my esophagus or my aorta?".

I prayed about it. My husband prayed out loud and asked the Lord, out loud.

The "Touch" revealed my aorta and blood flowing through it! Then He showed two separate, large platters. One was stacked with fruit and one was filled with vegetables! That's the answer

April 8, 2011 Listened again to Katie Souza's "Jesus, Curse Breaker". This is perhaps the third time! But I finally got it! I explained it to my husband and then asked him to look at me.

The "Touch" revealed the Lord, standing on swirling clouds. Behind Him were dark and storming clouds, billowing. In His right hand was the cross, lifted up. Wooden and plain and not very large. In His left hand were lightning bolts! Striking downward toward me! So we will see what happens next!

This evening the "Touch" revealed the Lord, still high up on a cloud. But no darkness behind Him, or anywhere. Right hand had a staff only. I take this as just to follow Him. That is what the staff represents.

April 9, 2011 I have been studying the effects of the radiation that I underwent ten years or so, ago. It's really bad for my aorta. After praying about it, the "Touch" revealed a fish. It was dripping oil. So that's it. Fish oil will help me.

April 10, 2011 This morning "Touch" revealed the Lord coming down a mountain trail. Both sides of the trail had large boulders. Behind the Lord was the little donkey, with no packs on its back. The Lord was almost running down the mountain trail! The little donkey could almost not keep up with Him! Almost at a run! I believe this is a serious change! Urgent for the Lord to move in this manner. We have never seen this before!

April 12, 2011 This morning the "Touch" revealed a shape of a large, golden heart. Flames of fire were coming from the center. Burning in the center and flaming upward, fanning upward and outward, larger than the heart area. Golden and red flames. Then a golden chalice overshadowed the entire area and only the chalice was seen. I will not attempt to interpret this???

April 13, 2011 Evening "Touch" revealed what appeared to be an eye, but it was not. It was a ship porthole. Looking through it you could see a vast ocean. A few ships here and there. ??

April 16, 2011 Evening "Touch" revealed looking over a cliff at the ocean below. Very, very high up on a cliff, looking downward at the water. ?

April 18, 2011 This noon time the "Touch" revealed two large cities. In between them was a vast body of water, like a vast river. This is three days of water showing! I have no idea what it means. This time I will ask in prayer and see what is revealed later today?

April 20, 2011 We asked the Lord about my book, in prayer. What should I do about not being able to write?

The "Touch" revealed the Lord, pointing downward, at something? Then He raised his hands as if beckoning to something? Very slowly and gently, the Holy Spirit, as a dove, came down and hovered, in His open hands. I told my husband that I did not understand what it meant. "Touch" me again. "Touch" revealed many people being baptized in a river. It looked as though I was among them. The Lord was on the bank of the river, receiving each one as they came out. His hand out to receive each one.

131

April 24, 2011 I seemed a little out of sorts for a few days. The "Touch" revealed one of my sons, standing. Very thin. Just standing. He had been ill and lost 55 pounds, but is on the road to recovery. I asked my husband to pray about it and let's ask what he is doing that hinders his recovery. The "Touch" revealed the huge letters spelling out:

"COFFEE"

Wow! That is amazing! We thanked God for such an answer. My son had been off coffee for a while, but was starting to drink it again. So we told him what the Touch had revealed!

May 8, 2011 I wanted to try a new church this Sunday. The pastor retired at the church I have been visiting for about 6 months. I drove around and saw the church that I had phoned for their hours of Sunday services. This is logging country and boy was I way over dressed! I felt so bad and out of place that I just kept driving. Then I was angry at myself for being so worried! I just drove on to the friendly little church that had no pastor. It was Mother's Day and the appointed visiting pastor's wife spoke for the service. She was pretty good! I enjoyed it.

May 11, 2011 This morning Touch, after prayer time, revealed a small church, with the cross on the side of the building, not above the building. Just attached to the front of the building. That is where I am to attend. I will look for the building and see if it is the one I have been going too?

May 15, 2011 Sunday morning and I am anxious to see if the church has the cross on the side of it? I went early. As I got close I could see the cross! On the side of the building! I practically ran in.

I asked in their office, if the pastor that was visiting was voted in?

They said, "yes".

I was glad that I knew and liked the pastor and his wife. Since I was early enough for the bible study class, I went on in. I settled in and paid attention to the speaker. After wards, as class broke up, I reintroduced myself to pastor's wife. I explained to her how happy I was that my husband saw, during prayer, this very church! For me to attend, with the cross on the side of the building, not on top! She said she had not even noticed. We chatted and then the service started. The pastor gave a teaching sermon on the book of Haggai.

After the service was over, he gave an altar call to all who would like to accept the Lord as their Savior. No one moved. That is not for me, I thought. Then he said, "You have given your life to the Lord, but have only laid the foundation and would like to build on the foundation?" That's not for me, I thought, I had a miraculous born-again experience with the Lord. No one moved. I decided I would wait for the next call. Again, he said, "You belong to the Lord and have not been walking with the Lord?" No one moved. That's not for me. I am walking with and hanging on to the Lord. Then he said, "Perhaps you would like to commit your life to the Lord or re-dedicate your self to the Lord." Well, that's really close for me. That's what I want, but I will wait and see what he says next. All of a sudden a hot heat was over my head! It came down through my head and went out over my shoulders and arms. I started to sweat and it covered my entire body. I was struggling. I wanted to get my coat off! A look from the pastors eyes to my eyes was like an arrow! But it was not the pastor. The Lord's face magnified through! It was super imposed in front of the pastor!

I saw anguish that was not of this world! I saw the eyes of the Lord just in front of the pastor!! The Holy Spirit was showing all feeling, for the lost! It was overwhelming and I sunk in the seat! I was weak and limp. The service was over. I tried to wait for the pastor to talk to him, but was not able to speak to him. I will keep trying to reach him.

May 18, 2011 I have a very hard time trying to write this book. I almost feel pain with writing. So I asked my husband if we could pray about the book. Should I just tell about the "Touch", or present time, or my life. The whole life? We prayed and the "Touch" revealed:

Me, a baby, as a toddler, young child and all stages. The whole thing. So I will do it. From the beginning to the end.

May 19, 2011 After praying, the "Touch" revealed that it was the Holy Spirit falling that caused the heat on me during Sunday's service.

May 24, 2011 Did not sleep well again! Can not fall asleep until around midnight! Consequently very tired after a few days of this. "Touch" this morning revealed white, yellow and blue lines in my brain. Moving and a lot of light, tiny lights sparkling? But I insisted to look further as to why I could not sleep. "Touch" showed that this particular energy made a cap on my head. Almost the same as my white hair, but just over and around my head. I again, asked what is it and all of it turned into a huge petaled flower. All of the flower was made of the same squiggly lines that were in side of my head??? I will just ponder on that? Within an hour I did go into heavy praise and prayer time. About 35 minutes. My knees were stiff when I tried to get up.

This time the "Touch" revealed a very large glass dome. The dome was made of glass triangles. I was seated inside. It could have been 30 to 40 feet high. The clouds were seen to pass by and overhead. Then a great white light shown through from above and

133

filled it all with a white light. I guess I had been writing this book. With my left arm, I powerfully closed the back of the book. Finished! It was over, completed, closed.

That's great! That means I will finish this book! I will get it completed and out there!

May 31, 2011 I asked my husband to pray with me about the book. I want to write it in an orderly way. But since I am not a writer, could I write it now as it happens? Could I finish up with my life and write this as present and whatever happens? The "Touch" revealed a tablet and on the top of the tablet was a tied, pack of arrows. Pointing to the right. I interpret this as go forward. Write pointing forward and straight arrow! Fly through it! I believe I am on track and with prayer, study and fellowship at the little church the Lord wants me to attend, there will be an outpouring of the Holy Spirit.

June 5, 2011 Sunday morning and I went to church very early, to look for my bible. I bumped into the pastor. I told him what I saw through him at the last service. He said it was in the word that the Lord did grieve for the lost. After service I was the first one to come forward to re-dedicate their walk.

June 12, 2011 Today the pastor asked me to speak to the church about what I saw and what was spoken into my heart last Sunday. I did and it was received very well.

June 14, 2011 I have been listening and watching John Paul Jackson and his prophecy. What he sees the United States going through in the tribulation period. I asked after prayer to see what the "Touch" revealed. There were four or five nuclear blasts. Then the dove flew toward each and they vanished! I do not even attempt to discern what it means. I will ask again, soon.

CORRECTION!

July 11, 2011 I have stopped writing for awhile now. Just a lot to mull over and understand. My daughter has had increasing problems after the birth of each child. One child is nine and the other is four and a half. She and her husband found an excellent doctor, locally. He is a psychiatrist and also a General practitioner. He has been a great help for therapy and medications. After a year of counseling, they began a search for my mother's records. My daughter's body chemistry and genetics are very much the same as my mother's.

The doctor contacted the hospital where my mother was a patient for almost 20 years. I was shocked to learn that he received her complete file! So after over seventy years, the file was still intact! My daughter and her doctor went over it during sessions with him.

I got very nervous about it. I asked if I could only be told a very little. During a visit with the grand-children and my daughter, she asked if I would like to see a pretty picture of my mother's face. I said "OK".

To my horror, I saw something in my mother's eyes that made my knees buckle!

"Don't show me any more photos! And I don't want to know too much, too fast!"

(My knees are shaking and so I'd take a break)

It is two days later and I am comfortable with writing.

My daughter explained to me some of the contents of the file.

When my mother was institutionalized in January of 1941, she had gone from postpartum psychosis, after delivery, to a schizophrenia state. This was a terrible tragedy for a young mother to go through. Then she endured multiple electric shock treatments. For me, the fact was uncovered, that she had 22 weekend, overnight visits, between 1941 and 1943. I was almost two at the time she would have started these weekend visits.

In the file, it was noted that a letter was received from, "the mother of the patient", my grandmother. She stated that "she feared for the children's safety". I assume that it was after some of these visits, that my Grandma took me.

I could feel a distant fear, when I would even think about the file. It will come up when I am frightened by someone that is irrational. I collapse and can not walk. My brain shuts off. I loose control of my bladder and bowels. I have wondered all my life why I would rather die than go through what happens to me.

And now I know the answer. The file tells it all. What the state of her illness was. The look in the eyes of my mother tells it all.

I did not go to live with my grandmother immediately after my mother was hospitalized. I was there for the weekend visits. All those visits, before my grandmother rescued me. I do remember when my mother broke an entire bedroom. I stood frozen. Dad could not hold her. She had the strength of ten people. I remember the baby in the bassinet and the neighbors coming in to clean and feed her. Then they would talk quietly to Dad, when he would come home. He was working nights. They always spoke in whispers.

But I couldn't reach what was wrong with me. That paralyzing fear spot in me. I have waited almost seventy years and feel it's OK to know now.

135

And so I prayed about it. I love my mom and feel she gave up her life, to have us, as her children. I am well and mature and have wisdom now. So I asked God to reveal it to me. What happened to me?

I asked my husband to pray about it, and "Touch" me.

The "Touch" revealed my father. His head was way back, and his mouth was fully opened. Screaming! His face was strained, like a weightlifter! His arms were pulling apart as hard as he could pull. Pulling and pulling apart my mothers arms. He was violently shaking and pulling! Pulling and pulling to save me. But I was already limp. She had cut my air off.

I have no conscious memory of this incident. But it fits somewhere in the deepest part of my soul.

My aunt told me of finding me under my mother, a few times. My mother screaming, that she was trying to protect me. Again, I was limp when they rescued me. She was seeing something that probably wasn't there.

I believe my grandmother took me at this time. My father must have realized that at two and a half, I was just too vulnerable.

To me, the puzzle pieces fit now. I can put it to rest. I understand and perhaps there is healing now. A lifetime later. How many people we judge for their actions. And some are just traumatized children? The wounded children. Even though I will take the wounds to the grave with me, I understand now. It's OK. I can bare it, with the Lord's help.

July 2011 I have been avoiding writing. Avoiding praying. Avoiding the "Touch". Sometimes I run from knowing things. But I always come back and try again. I have still been going to the very small, Spirit Filled, church. One morning, last week, the "Touch" revealed the pastor baptizing people. Everyone was lined up, with some urgency, to get baptized in water. I asked my husband to ask what it meant?

The "Touch" revealed the little church entirely consumed in fire! This entire two story building was completely engulfed in a teardrop shape of a fire, that reached above it by about two stories. Engulfed in a fire that consumed it but did not destroy it! I know it is the fire of God! It's what is called the "out pouring" of the Holy Spirit.

July 24, 2011 I went to church an hour early and waited for someone to arrive early. I was going to relate to the pastor a few things that I knew. But I couldn't. I tried and walked around and visited with everyone, but just couldn't talk to him.

August 2011 I have been praying, on my knees each day. And at night my husband and I pray together and bring each one of our seven children, and their spouses, before God. This is for over a year and a half now. There is a move of the Holy Spirit on some of them. One saw the face of the Lord magnified through a Christian friend and he was witnessed to. His life is changing. Praying every day now!!!!!

I am doing all of the DVD's and books from the Life Skills International. Paul Hegstrom teachings and CD's are the greatest tools for understanding the wounded child. I understand and can validate what the Lord did with me in healing. The trauma causes the wounded child to create a self that is detached from the hidden, real, inner self. You can no longer trust anyone or anything in your world. You are on your own to survive. But the wounded child makes all its own decision making from the wounded center. Most times at around three or four. You can not stop from being triggered and acting out or being self destructive. You are just functioning from the child's point, in the frozen center of the brain. The wounded, false self, can sin, be self destructive, commit crime, drink and cheat. Nothing matters because the spirit and higher self is frozen in time. But there is a way back. Putting the two back together, with the help of God, prayer and learning. It is a miracle of the Spirit and so simple and easy. But so few find it. The young are stolen by the enemy and live such pain. To be living separate from the presence of God within. But if they make it back to themselves, the reward is the waiting glory of God. They get to feel the self inside again. They get to know the presence of God again! It is glorious!

"The bigger the mess, the greater the message", as Paul Hegstrom stated!

The brain will respond to truth spoken out loud. But it has to be from your own voice. Your brain will only listen to you. So you can only take in the sound of your own voice. Read the new testament, to start, feel and hear and understand in your spirit what you are reading. You will recognize truth, then speak it to your self, what is truth. Repeat it, out loud, often. Meditation on quieting the self, being still, will send you back to yourself.

I just stopped writing and asked my husband to "Touch" my head. The "Touch" revealed the Lord Jesus Christ, sitting. Reading a book! My book!

I stopped everything and prayed. I cried and cried. I think this book is finished? Or just about? I regret that I am not a writer. That I can not explain everything enough, to be perfectly, helpful. But I have told the truth. As God would have it. Not man. It does not weigh in the finishing of the book, that it might not be believed. It took a long life for me to understand my injury. If I can help someone find their way back to their self, I will smile. God will smile on you. The Lord Jesus Christ is waiting for you to speak the living word to your self. It will heal you.

End of August 2011. The "Touch" revealed the eastern sky, splitting open! Clouds rolling apart and the Holy Spirit as a Dove, as big as the whole sky, in the center, as the

137

sky rolled apart! I don't know what it means?

Sept. 2011 The "Touch" revealed the Lord standing, in a bright haze of light. In a white robe, with His arms reaching upward, hands open. I was in a cave, looking out toward the Lord. The rounded edges of the entrance could be seen. As if looking outward. Just above the Lord's hands was the "Touch". The Holy Spirit.

I do not know or feel what this means?

September 15, 2011 I asked the question of the Lord, "is it that I can not, at this time, receive the full baptism of the Holy Spirit"?

I am supposing, that during the writing of this book, it is necessary for me to be feeling what happened in my early life. The feelings are still raw and some are buried deep in my sub-conscience. I do not understand everything at this time.

This morning the "Touch" revealed me sleeping, stirring a little. While sleeping on my back, the Dove, The Holy Spirit came with a great light and touched my forehead. Then as it moved upward, and away, a flame as in the shape of a tear drop, was left at my forehead. It was about a foot tall. Perhaps this will be in the future. I am satisfied with the answer, and will step up the writing of the early years.

October 4, 2011 I have not been writing, as the early childhood emotions come up as the problems are told and exposed. I am not sleeping very well and have not been able to rest for a long time. Always when I ask why, the Touch reveals a lot of high energy inside my head. I have never understood what the energy was. So last night I asked the Lord, why is it that I can sleep soundly in San Francisco? Deep sleep and can sleep through the night? But in my bedroom, I can not sleep soundly and through the night? I know there is huge energy in my head, but what is the problem? "Pray about it and Touch me" I said to my husband.

The "Touch" revealed my telephone. I'd had it for over nine or ten years! It is a Uniden digital answering system, 900 MHz! The huge PG&E box is on the outside wall next to the head of our bed and my pillow. We moved the bed to another wall.

I went to bed and slept like a brick! Slept through the whole night!

This morning I asked what the "Touch" revealed? Since I slept through!

Almost the same as two weeks ago, Sept. 15th, I was sleeping. Above my forehead was a large flame, in the same teardrop shape! Above the flame, and a little distance, was the Holy Spirit as the Dove! This is Good! It's wonderful. I don't know what it means or what I will experience, but I know it is Great!!!

So I am trying to write again!

October 20, 2011 Very early this morning the "Touch" revealed my oldest son, as a toddler. He was playing and running around. Perhaps around 3 1/2 years old. I know this is where the Lord wants to heal him. I know, and understand now, the words of the Lord. "must be born again". When you are injured, traumatized and wounded, you die a death. The brain freezes. God will go back and get you, if you let Him. You just have to be willing. I do understand now, for myself and others.

Michael and I asked the Lord if I can tell the truth, the whole truth, to this son. The Lord revealed His Face, magnified through a person, to this son and his heart must be ready to hear what I have been learning.

The "Touch" revealed in big capital letters! The first spelling out of letters since April!!

"IT'S TIME"

Michael was shocked and surprised at the letters being shown. The letters appear to Michael very quickly and then vanish! I have to write or jot down a record as fast as I can. This was similar to the moving letters noted in this book on January 26th.

I have been unable to write. I have started praying again, just a little. As soon as I am on my knees and begin praying out loud, or thanking God for things and events, the power of God falls on me. It's so big that everything in me is charged! My cheeks hurt the most! I would say that around four minutes after beginning, the power falls on me. It is huge!

"God inhabits the praises of His people!" It's true!!. I stopped praying and praising in the 1980's because I did not know what it was that was hurting me. Now I understand that I am just human and the power is Divine. I am inadequate to be before it!

I asked my husband to pray about this issue and "Touch" my head.

He did. It was confirmed by God, revealing that the huge power falls. It appears yellow-golden-white, then changes to blue-white.

My husband said, "makes my face glow as it comes toward me". That is what causes the pain.

October 27, 2011 I have been trying not to be in a spirit of guilt. Guilt over the youthful days of my past. Before I met the Lord and was saved. After praying about it and studying the subject, I was aware in my spirit, that I was wrong to do this. Live in the feeling of guilt. Everything was paid for with the Lamb of God. Writing this book brings it all back. It's painful, and then I move on and continue writing. I asked my husband to pray about it and I would ask the Lord about it.

The "Touch" revealed, in big, capital letters!

"FALSE GUILT!"

I was to be under Grace! Not under Guilt!

I said that I understood. But I asked, "is this so important?"

The "Touch" revealed, in big, capital, letters:

"FOR THE LOVE OF GOD"

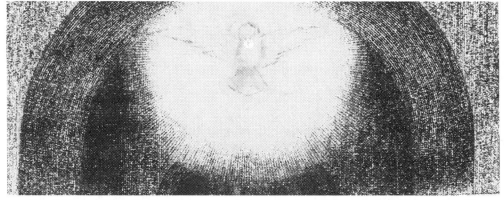

Holy Spirit, as a Dove glowing golden, was known by early artists and those that could see in the spirit.

That answer can mean many things, to many people. To me it means, under Grace, there is an open door to Heaven. I can love God. Direct my love toward God. The open door of Grace can let the love of God be upon me. So I am satisfied that I can stay away from guilt. I understand. I try each day to stop the guilt.

October 28, 2011 I prayed this morning. I have always wondered why it is different now, than immediately after, I was saved? That the first few weeks and months, after I met the Lord, The Presence was profound! I could almost Touch Him! The presence! I asked my husband to pray about it and I would too. The "Touch" revealed the words in capitals!

"LOST SOUL"

Well I understand now! I came from an agonizing lost soul, to a saved and loved soul! The presence was felt because the change was so profound! That was fifty or so years ago and now I am used to belonging to the Lord.

So I asked again, "I need to do anything? Is there anything that is needed?"

I asked my husband to Touch me and I said it again, out loud. The "Touch" revealed, in big capital letters:

"NOT SINCE I SPOKE TO YOU!"

Wow! Everything was done! He did everything! He gave everything. It's completed. I have nothing to say or ask. It's as though it was yesterday and it was nearly fifty years ago. Nothing needed! The Lord Jesus Christ would mention speaking to me and it was a lifetime ago. But it feels like a moment ago, he spoke!

Nov. 1, 2011 I have studied for many, many years about the end times. Who is the anti-Christ? Who is the false prophet and the ten nations? So this morning I drew a very detailed drawing of the end times. A big Catholic Church and the head of it as the false prophet! I drew the mountains and told my husband that the mountains were the nations and I named them! I felt so sure about everything I was stating as a fact! Catholic Church is going to align with and be the head of it all, I said. Then I said lets pray about it. We did and then I asked my husband to "Touch" me.

Big capital letters!

"NO"

The wind went out of my theory. I was completely wrong! So I went on and cleaned the house and just thought about it. But I was very surprised!

So in the afternoon, I sat down with my husband, and explained how surprised I was to be so wrong. So I asked, then where will the false prophet and the anti-Christ come from? Let's ask the Lord. After praying for a few moments, my husband touched my head.

Immediately there appeared a large area in gray and black and white. A crescent moon with a star inside it! There was no color at all. Only gray, white and black. So I do not know which country it was, but I feel it was symbolic of Muslim or Islam. The false prophet and the anti Christ will come out of Islam. It is for sure. God does not make any mistakes.

November 5, 2011 My husband and I sit and pray for all the needs of our seven adult children, the grandchildren and anyone we have been asked to pray for. We hold them in prayer every night before we go to sleep. We have been watching each night, and as I lay my head down on the pillow, the Holy Spirit as the Dove is about a foot above me. The days go by now, and The Spirit does not move away from me. I asked the Lord, what should I do about the Holy Spirit above me? I prayed about it and asked my husband to "Touch" my head. The words:

"BE THANKFUL."

So that is all I know at this time, about the Holy Spirit above me.

November 7, 2011 While listening to my CD's on the New Testament, "door" was brought to my attention again.

The Lord said "You will see me in the face of everyone that comes through the door". Well, that was 45 years ago. I have not been able to see His face again, although I am still trying. So I am working at understanding it. I study and study all scripture on this subject. My husband and I tossed around ideas of what it means. We concluded that you hear the voice of the Lord inside, inside the heart of your spirit. I have heard the voice. You never forget what is said to you, from God. It never leaves you. There is no time in the voice. Time stops when you hear. So finally I felt that I needed to ask.

I asked my husband to "Touch" my head after I prayed about it.

I asked, "who opens the door? Can anyone open the door? How do you open the door?"

The "Touch" revealed:

"KNOCK" in big letters again. Always big letters now.

I was in awe and did not know what to think! I had to just walk around and ponder and think! Sometimes I feel as though I just don't understand so much that is being revealed to me. Even though the Lord is trying to tell me in easy and plain words. So I cleaned the kitchen and worked for some time.

I sat down with my husband and we went over our thoughts about the "Touch". Jesus being the "Touch". Some scripture states that the Lord is knocking and some scripture asks the person to knock. So both are valid.

"I am missing something. I don't understand. What should I do? What am I missing, in not being able to understand. What should I do, to hear? How can I hear the knock? What is missing?"
We prayed out loud and asked the Lord again, these exact questions.

142

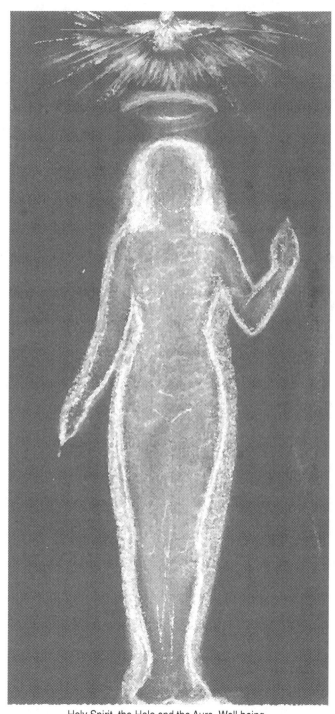

Holy Spirit, the Halo and the Aura. Well being.

143

My husband touched my head and in big capital letters:

"BELIEVE TRUST LOVE"

There it is! I do believe because the Lord snatched me from death! I love as much as I can and try to do better. But it is the trust issue. I think my injuries as a baby and toddler have made it difficult. I still have trouble with the Lord fixing things and me not directing the show. It is fear based and it comes upon me. But I will keep learning and try again! Push forward. Praise and pray and work it through!. The voice of the Lord, as He speaks, goes directly into the heart. You hear with your heart. The Lord speaks, and when the heart is right, you hear. I have heard Him speak, a long time ago.

November 8, 2011. I am going to tell the end now. I believe there is only a few things more to tell. If you read this, read very slowly. This last part, if it is the end of this book, is difficult to understand? I have gone to the deepest pit of hell, and then to the Presence of God. So that might have made me able to bear what the Lord now shows.

Earlier in this book, the Lord showed dead whales on a beach. I do not know where it took place. I have been very concerned over Fukushima and also any other nuclear disaster.

After praying this morning, the "Touch" revealed:

Me, carrying a medium size box of food? Putting food away in the cupboard?

I needed to know what it meant! Was it related to what was written and revealed earlier in this book? I asked my husband to please let me ask again! So we talked it over and clarified what we were praying about and asking about. The box of food?

He touched my head and it revealed:

A mist.

It appeared as a fog. Moving through the tops of the trees. Then the mist, or rain fog, moved across great expanses of fields of grain or wheat? Great fields of food! It all became contaminated!

My thinking is that the mist, or fog, will cause a famine or at least food shortages! I think it is some kind of fallout?

So I asked "Is the Rapture before the famine?"

The "Touch" revealed:

144

"ONLY TIME WILL TELL."

I take that to mean that mankind could restrain their nuclear recklessness?? I just don't know and it's too big for my mind just now!

I couldn't think anymore. I just wanted to clean house and try to take this into my mind and spirit!

But after an hour or so, I wanted to press in and learn more! What can we do? What should we do? Is there anything we can do? Again, we prayed and talked about it.

And so my husband touched my head.

The Lord revealed the plastic greenhouses. They were long. You see them in the magazines and on line. The rounded PVC pipe type. With plastic covering! I take that to mean that, while the fog or mist is deadly to crops, food can be still grown in the greenhouses! That is exciting! If there is time. If anyone would ever believe me.

But this book I am writing? What about my book? Is there time? So I asked again.

"What about my book?"

The "Touch" revealed the words:

"IT IS UP TO YOU."

So I take that to mean that the time of problems to come, is not set in stone. No one knows. I can not write that fast and complete this book within days. But I will work harder at it!

I asked if I could tell people about the need to grow food in protected greenhouses?. Could I tell people to prepare to have a food supply? It just seems like such a big project! Perhaps no one will believe me! So, my husband and I talked it over and clarified what we were going to ask.

The clear question is, can I tell people? The "Touch" revealed, in capital letters:

"YOU CAN SHARE."

I am comfortable with that answer. And I will try talk to some people. I can see the point of this book as it draws to an end. But I wanted to know the Lord's thought. So I talked with my husband about the end of the book and the meaning of the book.

145

We asked in prayer, "What is the meaning of the book?"

The big capital letters were:

"KNOWLEDGE"

So, it is about knowledge. Knowledge of the healing of the Lord and the love of the Lord. That the Lord would show greenhouses ahead of time! We are still ahead of time! With knowledge we could be prepared. Some of the dome greenhouses are huge. If our government would start to experiment with food production in the greenhouse domes, we could survive a contamination of our food. Other countries could prepare!

As we were getting ready to go to sleep. I told my husband that I hoped I could interpret everything accurately and do a good job. We prayed about it and the "Touch" revealed:

"KEEP WRITING."

And so I will.

December 16, 2011 I was just telling my husband that no one could tell when this time of trouble will come. Perhaps in a year, in ten years or twenty! I guess all things are flexible? Maybe it could be postponed? Maybe no one knows! I went on and on about my view on this subject, of contamination by fallout. When I was all through with my speech, I asked my husband to "Touch" my head.

The big capital letters showed:

"YOU KNOW."

We are shocked! I'd know! That's big. My concern is regarding the greenhouses. I can see on line that people are posting high radiation readings in Canada! Hopefully, there is nothing to it, at this time. But, I will know when it will be. I don't understand at this time? But I will know, when the time comes.

December 17, 2011 I am writing as fast as I can now. I feel it is almost urgent to finish. This morning we talked about the book. Who would help me? Is there someone out there to help me publish it? Where should I go to find someone to help? So we talked and talked and prayed about it. He touched my head and asked "Will help?"

The "Touch" revealed:

"WHEN IT'S TIME YOU WILL FIND SOMEONE."

So I guess it's up to me.

December 19, 2011 This morning, after coffee, I tried to convince my husband that we needed a large, dome greenhouse. He didn't like the idea. Too much work! And it got into which might be the best, PVC or steel? Well, we just went in circles about it. So, I reminded him that the Lord Himself, was the one to show us about the mist moving across the agricultural lands. The food that was contaminated by the fallout? At least I believe that was what was meant, when it showed food grown under plastic coverings. I thought it was from Fukushima? So I went on and on, thinking, that I was meant to have a greenhouse. I asked my husband to pray about it and "Touch" my head.

He did, and it revealed the words:

"FREE WILL"

Well, that just doesn't make sense to me. If there is contamination by fallout, and I can grow food under plastic, wouldn't I need to have a greenhouse?

I explained to my husband that I couldn't understand, and Touch my head again. And the words were the same!

"FREE WILL"

Well, OK. I can have a greenhouse if I want one. That is my free will. OK. I understand that. But something is wrong here. I told my husband that I must be miss-understanding about the fog or mist from Fukushima?

"I have to know and understand this point accurately. It would be a terrible mistake to write in my book, if I am way off!" If we don't need the greenhouse, then I am not getting it right! Please, let's ask what am I miss interpreting?"

So my husband touched my head. I'll be as careful, as I can, to explain it.

What he saw in my head, was the earth, turning. The entire earth. Then it focused in, on the area of the border between Pakistan and India. Almost dead center was Lahore, near the border. Right there was almost dead center. The pronounced area of a circle, extended north to Karaganda, Kazakhstan, west to Tehran, Iran, south to Madras, India, east to, almost, Chengdu, China. I put a clear glass circle, on top of the map, to try to be accurate, over what my husband saw, with the "Touch" to my head.

So I did have it all wrong! I jumped to conclusions that it was Fukushima. I needed to know more.

So I asked, out loud, "the mist, fog or fallout contamination, of this whole area?"

I asked my husband to ask it in prayer, when he touched my head. The answer was:

"IT COULD IT MAY IT MIGHT"

I needed to just gather my thoughts together. It is hard for me to take all this into my mind. To me it meant that mankind was deciding his own destiny. If the Lord said, "could". So I started going on and on to my husband about the book of Revelation. Maybe I am reading that wrong too? I seem to be getting everything wrong. So I wanted to know if mankind was able to stop this devastation? Was mankind choosing this? My husband and I talked a bit, and then he touched my head. The "Touch" revealed:

"MY WILL WILL BE DONE"

"THY WILL WILL BE DONE"

I am not going to try to go any further on this subject at this time. I am going to leave this as it is.

Christmas Day, 2011 I have not written for a few days. Just gathering my thoughts and spending some time with grandchildren.

About three or four years ago, I'll figure it out later, I was studying intensely, about Jewish Mysticism and the old and new Testament. Months turned into a year! Everything I could get my hands on. Tapes, books, CD's and some DVD's. I could discern any and all untruth within different theories. With a half hour of meditation, on the Word of God, on quieting down and settling down, each day, I was really feeling good! Positive and calm and together! I was super woman! I thought I knew almost everything!

I was sitting on the couch, alone in the house, just looking out at the garden. It was beautiful. Suddenly, toward the upper right side of my vision area, it was moving. I blinked! There was a large circle taking about one fourth of my visual area! Within this large area, it was vibrating in triangular shapes! All things that I would see normally, within this area, was moving in triangular or diamond shapes! Pulsating! I jumped up and hit myself on the side of the face, near my eye to stop it! I thought I might go blind! I ran to the bedroom and looked in the mirror! I couldn't see anything strange in my eye! But the large circle area was still pulsating in triangles! I sat down on the bed and was going to cry. I closed my eyes and was amazed to see that it was there with my eyes closed! I thought perhaps I'm dying! I opened my eyes and it was still there! Big and white and bright triangles, pulsating! I smacked myself upside my head a few more times and eventually, it stopped.

I was so unnerved by the incident, that I stopped everything for a time. All studies put on hold!

At this period of time, I was visiting my oldest son, each month, in San Francisco. He had suffered when I was a very young woman, and divorced. During a visit, it became apparent how much he was suffering and hurting, still. I was devastated by the fact that I could not help him! I had no power! I had nothing to mend him with. I had no knowledge of how to help to heal him! I had no miracles! I was driven back to my knees and to my God. And so began the very slow journey of learning how childhood wounds cripple and affect even the brain chemicals.

The Lord took me by the hand and showed me the way back, for the wounded. And so I asked "Why am I so aware of the wounds to myself and my son, now? At this late date in time. This long journey backwards, in time?"

The "Touch" revealed:

"TO SETTLE THINGS THAT WERE UNSETTLED."

And then more was written out in the "Touch":

"FOR YOUR GUILT AND THE LOVE OF YOUR SON."

And so we talked it over and again, I asked my husband, out loud,

"Am I doing it, Lord? Am I working at it and doing it right? Am I learning the way back for my son?"

Michael touched my head and the "Touch" revealed:

"EFFICIENTLY"

That is just wonderful and I will keep going and am on track with all that I am learning!

December 26, 2011 I told my husband that I wanted to know about the circle of triangles and thinking I was going blind. "Why did it happen?"

The "Touch" revealed:

"TO GET MY ATTENTION"

I asked again, "Why?"

The "Touch" revealed:

"TO UNDERSTAND"

149

"But what was it that I needed to understand?" The "Touch" revealed:

"MISGIVINGS"

I didn't really know the exact and correct meaning of misgivings, so I looked it up. It means "presentiment or premonition of evil; a state of apprehension."

That has been my state since my early childhood. I now understand. As painful as it has been, I have been exposed to the truth about my wounds and how they affect me. I understand more about other people that are wounded. The study is slow going and is slowly unfolding.

So I asked again, "Why?" The "Touch" revealed:

"BENEFICIAL"

Full Holy Spirit position. Halo just above the aura. Sometimes touching and moving by love.

And it has been beneficial. Exposing the truth of the wounds. Exposing my reaction to fear as a trigger, even presently. The need to forgive so the brain can heal. Slowing down the reaction time of any trigger. But the greatest aid is the Lord leading through the healing! What to study. How to pray and praise. How to incorporate the Holy Spirit into the healing and mending. I am just at the point of understanding a great principle on healing. I am not there yet, but I can feel how close I am!

I needed to know one more thing. It has been an unfolding and learning experience. But one issue is very disputed. Meditation. But my way of meditation is different. I settle down and sit in a chair or anywhere, comfortable and quiet. Takes me a while to settle down. I do not zone out or go anyplace. With my eyes closed, I get quieter and quieter. My hands are open and relaxed, placed on my legs, palms upward. I very slowly, say, only in my mind, quietly, "I praise you Lord God Jehovah, I Praise the name of Jesus Christ Messiah, the Lamb of God." I can change this prayer statement, but the same attitude is maintained. All the while, perhaps a half hour, becoming still. To be still inside, deep in the quiet place. This is very different than powerful, out loud, praise!

And so the question of Meditation was discussed with my husband. I asked if meditation was helpful? Was it good to meditate? Specifically, the way I was doing meditation? The question was asked, out loud, if meditation was good? The "Touch" revealed:

"DEFINITELY"

So I put this to rest.

December 27, 2011 I was out of town for a few days, with family. We all went to the movies. I knew right away, that even from the sound track, this might be a movie too hard on my spirit. But I was too embarrassed to suggest leaving. I thought I could handle it without any problems to my spirit. A violent and sexually perverted movie. I covered my eyes and ears during the worst of it. I felt that I might be in trouble. So I prayed and meditated that night and the next day. When I arrived home, I asked my husband to take a look at me. My halo was dark and small. The circle above me that had the Holy Spirit Dove above me, was almost gone. It had moved away from me. I felt terrible and sorry. I asked my husband to pray about it and Touch my head and ask, "What should I do?"

The "Touch" revealed:

"REPENT"

So I did. I said how sorry I was. I would learn from this. I wouldn't do it again and I'd be more careful. I prayed about it. Meditated about it and thanked God that I could be repentant. By the time I laid my head on the pillow, to go off to sleep, the Holy Spirit as the Dove was over me and was back to bright and large and close! I was so thankful!

151

I asked my husband to Touch my head. He saw the words.....

"REMEMBER WHATEVER YOU LET INTO YOUR MIND OR HEART. I AM THERE."

"I AM WITH YOU ALWAYS."

I will be more careful for myself and be more discerning.

NEW YEAR'S DAY The "Touch" revealed:

"WHAT WILL BE WILL BE."

I don't know why that disturbs me so much? But it does disturb me! I won't think about it.

JANUARY 2, 2012 Things are quieting down now, after the Holidays. I have not been writing for a few days. This morning the "Touch" revealed:

"TEN COMMANDMENTS FOLLOW HONOR RESPECT"

So I will do that. I will do my best. Actually, I will look them over, as I don't have them memorized.

I have decided to start drawings of what we can see. Or I should say, what my husband can see. I am just the one that the Lord can use to explain what He wants... Only my husband can "see".

January 15, 2012 Sunday morning the pastor held the service, a little different. We were singing praise songs and worshiping all together. Then we all received communion. Pastor said he would like to just continue on with the praise singing, for a time. Just sing and worship the Lord. And so we did. It was just great singing. I was trying to relax and get into the worship time. But I was in the front row and trying not to be self conscious! So I closed my eyes and continued singing. And the sounds of everyone singing was beautiful. Within a short period of time, with my eyes still closed, light appeared. Light that was growing, lighter and lighter, upward, inside my closed eyes! Brighter and brighter and bigger and bigger, was light! It caused my arms to stretch toward the light! It was as though my self was reaching toward it! My arms were beginning to tremble! It was powerful and overwhelming. A glorious all encompassing light! I thought I might fall down and die. I did fall down in my seat, in shock! I got my composure back and did not know if anyone saw my arms shaking! I guess no one else saw the light?

152

After the service I tried to tell the Pastor what happened. It was awkward and he did not understand. So I left and drove home. On the way, I noticed that my face was burned. Very similar to the face burn 45 years ago when I went into the blinding light.

When I got home, I explained, as best I could, to my husband, what had happened. I needed to understand and write about it. We talked it over and asked what happened. The "Touch" revealed:

The Holy Spirit as a Dove, within a light, glowing and radiating circle. Huge! Beams of light shooting outwards.

"But why? Why did it happen now? What is different?"

The "Touch" revealed:

"DEVOTION"

So I will just think about that today. I'll rest and think about it until tomorrow.

January 16, 2012 This morning we talked about the light that I experienced. I needed to know more if I was going write about it.

So out loud, I asked "I don't understand?" The "Touch" revealed:

"JESUS STANDING WITH HIS ARMS OPEN, AS IF RECEIVING OUR DEVOTION"

"IN THE CENTER OF HIS CHEST AREA WAS HIS HEART WITHIN A RADIATING LIGHT. BEAMS WERE EMANATING OUTWARD FROM HIS HEART AREA"!

I then knew what had happened. Our praise singing was the DEVOTION that the Lord received. Our Love to Him. It brought the Glory of God into our midst! I knew exactly what had happened now. A few months earlier, I think I put it into this book, we saw this entire church consumed in fire. A fire that did not destroy the building. I know it was the Glory of God! That's what I saw!

January 17, 2012 I have thought about how this all works, with the "Touch".

So my conclusion is that the Lord shows me something. I try to understand. Then I write it down in this book. Then in a matter of time, not my time, but the Lord's time, it will happen. I don't expect it. Sometimes I don't recognize it. But eventually it matches to what has been shown to me.

So I talked it over with my husband and I asked the question, out loud.

"Is this true Lord?" Am I perceiving it all correctly?" The "Touch" revealed:

"YES"

January 24, 2012 I found, quite by accident, that the royal family that my Grandma talked about is all recorded. It's all laid out. It's all there. There are 4000 in my tree already and I have to stop. All go back to Bran the Blessed, The Fisher King, Joseph of Arimathea and Beli Mawr. I had to stop after I tried many different paths and there was just too much. But it was interesting. It just took too much of my time and I would not write this book. And this is my priority!

This came as a surprise to me, that it would be recorded so far back. I am going to tell most of what I have learned about this. I will keep a few facts private. Facts that would involve no one else but me. Questions that I asked the Lord. He answered me and it was very kind of Him to do so.

I asked why was it shown to me, about the linage of my family? I discussed it with my husband, so we would both be asking the Lord the same question. The "Touch" revealed:

"YOUR MANIFEST"

I didn't know the correct meaning, so I looked it up. It means the record. Clear, plain or apparent. The record. The record of my family. I asked about this book. Where is it going? I don't understand that much? We talked it over and the "Touch" revealed, a picture of the Ten Commandments, then it showed the Bible and then it spelled:

"FREE WILL"

I have the free will to write what ever I will. Whatever I want to write! I have to interpret what is shown to me. Or how I perceive, what I am told. It is my conclusion.

So I explained to my husband that I can't write! I have to try to understand where the book is going? Let's ask. One more time, lets ask about the book. The "Touch" revealed:
"FOLLOW YOUR HEART."

January 25, 2012 I am always asking about this book and what to write. Sometimes it is easy and sometimes hard. I continue my prayer time each day and my studies. Studies in the Bible and studies of the wounded children and healing. I talked with my husband of my concerns of the wounds of childhood.

I said out loud, "I don't understand childhood injuries and a lifetime, life line, play out? And then the healing???" I asked my husband to "Touch" me, as I had asked this question out loud. The "Touch" revealed:

"YOU WILL."

"STUDY AND UNDERSTAND."

January 27, 2012 Many times I will ask a question, perhaps silly, and there is nothing. No answer. So I try to write and not ask silly or shallow questions of life.

The Knights Templar have been shown to me for this past year. When I ask what does it mean? The answer from the "Touch" is always the same:

"IN TIME."

In time I will understand what it all means. This is a little step of understanding and then another little tiny step of understanding of spiritual unfolding of mysteries. Mysteries of this end time that the Lord wants all to understand.

The Lion of Judah and the Knights Templar were shown earlier in this book. The Templar shield with the red cross is shown to me often. The Lion of Judah is also shown often. So I asked the Lord, what am I connected to. It always shows up? Is it the Lion of Judah that I am connected to, or is it the Knights Templar that I am connected to? We talked it over, out loud, so there would be no misunderstanding of the issue in question. Which one was I related to? The Touch revealed:

"BOTH"

I didn't want to ask anything else.

February 1, 2012 I talked to my husband about the book. About my concerns of the wounds of childhood. My lifetime of study of God and religion and meditation. Do I know enough? Do I have enough experience to complete the book? Can I go on alone? Can I search with the guidance of the Holy Spirit?

"Let's ask out loud. Let's both pray and ask if I can go on?"

The "Touch" revealed:

"YOU HAVE ENOUGH KNOWLEDGE."

February 3, 2012 I just asked if I could write about the Grail gift. If I could write

155

about my husbands vision and his dream. I discussed it just now with my husband. I asked again, out loud if it was OK to write about it? The "Touch" revealed:

"YES"

So I will try. If you are reading this book, then you already know I am not a writer. I stumble through and do my best.

One of my son's, my oldest son, recently saw, the Face of the Lord Jesus Christ, magnified through a person. It has changed his life and his belief in God. Manifested, just the same, as the way, I saw the Face of Jesus Christ. Most of our family does not know about this.

The Holy Grail is the Shed Blood of the Lamb of God. Jesus Christ

The Holy Grail is the shed Blood of Christ Jesus.

I felt this is very, very important! I don't want to miss-understand this very important issue. So I asked, is this the Grail?

The "Touch" revealed these exact words:

"IT'S HOW YOU LOOK AT IT."

Then slowly written:

"AS YOU LOOK AT IT"

That's it. It is within the eye of the beholder! I will pray about it and I will correct any statement, where I am wrong or have made a mistake. I will be careful!

I just asked if I got it right? Did I do OK? The "Touch" revealed:

OK

I am going to stop writing now. I feel, in time, I will have a better understanding of this important issue. I will wait on what is to be revealed.

Chapter Twenty-Three

Trying to Finish

I am going to try to finish this book quickly. I am old now and anything could happen? It might be sloppy and perhaps a little hard to read. But the hidden messages, behind the words, are what is important.

At this time there is a great outpouring of the Holy Spirit. As the praise music is sung in our little tiny congregation, the Holy Spirit falls! It is so huge, light and golden, glorious above the people! I am going to try to find out if anyone else experiences it! The Touch did reveal to my husband and me, that I am only to talk to my pastor now. Just him, at this time. The Lord did tell us that it is up to me to get this book out. As quickly as I can.

Here is the reason.

It was explained, earlier in this book, that a nuclear accident in the area of the border between Pakistan and India, would cause fallout. That food could be grown in greenhouses. Large greenhouses and small, low, long green house plastic covers over the rows of food outside. It could be done. It should be done!

I have been afraid to ask the Lord about a lot of things. But all day, yesterday, I had something on my mind. The scales in the hand of the rider on the black horse, in Revelation 6? I talked it over with my husband and what it might mean?

I said, "I wonder what is the significance of the scales? What could it mean?"

We talked about it and I asked, out loud, "what are the scales in the hand of the rider on the black horse, in Revelation?"

I told my husband to ask in prayer and the "Touch" revealed a picture.

The picture was of a pile of gold coins and silver coins and paper money. It was on one side of the scale. It was over a foot high.

On the other side of the scale was a little bit of food. A tiny bit of food!

We did a drawing of it. I didn't ask anything else. I didn't want to know anything else.

February 14th, 2012 I am usually writing as fast as I can. So I took a break. I wanted to know if the scales with wealth on one side and tiny bit of food on the other side had anything to do with the border between Pakistan and India? I talked it over with my husband and asked him to Touch my head. The "Touch" revealed:

"ONLY TIME WILL TELL...."

I know enough, of how this works now, that it means free will!

February 16, 2012 I felt confused about the accident on the border area between India and Pakistan. I am confused about the contaminated areas? So I talked it over with my husband. I tried to clarify what I was questioning and asking. We discussed it at length. Then I asked out loud,

"Will the contamination of the accident, near the border in India, reach the USA?"
My husband put his hand on my head and the "Touch" revealed:

"DEPENDING ON THE FACILITY"

I looked at my husband, amazed, and asked out loud,

"Do you mean a nuclear reactor?"

My husband touched my head again, after I asked out loud. The "Touch" revealed:

"YES"

I tried to write, just now, that the balances in the hand of the rider on the black

158

horse, were related to food shortages. The large pile of gold and silver on one side and the tiny bit of food, balanced on the other side of the scale. I thought it was caused by the nuclear accident. I was just corrected!. Had to take it out of this page. I asked and tried to understand. The "Touch" revealed:

"YOUR THEORY"

So I was wrong. I misunderstood about the greenhouses and food and such? I will not write this book on my personal theories. It has to be correct. So I said I would stop writing if I couldn't get it straight!

So the greenhouses and the weights and balances might not be connected? I do not know or understand? I told my husband, out loud, that, "I do not understand and will not use my theories!"

I asked, "Can we pray about it and you Touch my head and see if we can get an answer that I understand?"

The "Touch" revealed:

"SEVERE ACCIDENT"

I have to leave it at that. I can not ask anymore. I don't think there is anything more to know. After we prayed for all our kids and their families, my husband prayed over me. When he touched my head, the little donkey appeared. Little donkey was pulling a very small cart. He was almost to the top of a steep mountain. I might be a little stubborn like a donkey! First time the donkey has appeared in over a year!!

I'm not going to write for a while. I went to bed and cried and cried about this book. Finally, I fell asleep.

February 24, 2012 I cried when I got up this morning.

But during the evening I went back over my writing. I read Revelation 6, and suddenly, I began to understand! Then the answer came to me. It's there and very clear. We are not at the time of the opening of the seals! We are not at the time of the four horsemen of Revelation! That is another time. I thought they were tied together because of danger to the growing of food! But it has no connection! That is why the Lord said:

"YOUR THEORY"

It was just my theory! What a mistake! I ran to tell my husband that I had found the interpretation mistake! I explained it to him.

Then I prayed out loud, "the nuclear accident is different than the weights and balances of the rider on the black horse? That is of another time? I was wrong, my theory was wrong!"

My husband touched my head and the "Touch" revealed:

"YES"

I have it right this time! It is an accident. A severe accident. But not related to the breaking of the seals and the four horsemen! Not related to the scales and balances! That is another time! More distant, in the future!

"IN TIME"

February 25, 2012 I want to finish up this book. I have decided to write a second book of what will be, this next year. Or perhaps have a website to keep up what I learn. To try to keep it currant. But in finishing up, I have to, sort of sum up what I know.

So just now, I asked my husband if we could pray about the Holy Spirit. Could we ask the Lord if I am allowed to write about the Holy Spirit?

"Would you ask out loud? Please. I don't want to do any writing that I am not supposed to write!"

And so my husband asked out loud and then he touched my head. The "Touch" revealed:

"ONLY WHAT YOU KNOW"

That is wonderful! Then I won't do any of my theories and make mistakes! I am learning to be careful!

So here goes! And I will include drawings of this wonderful and glorious part of this unfolding!

A few weeks or months back, my husband began to notice, a circle of light above my halo. It could have been there for some time. But usually we just check my aura, my halo and my chest area where the cancer was. So once he noticed the circle above my halo, we began to watch more closely. Sometimes the rays of light emanating out of the circle grew stronger. Each day he could see the Dove Holy Spirit clearly. We watch now and it does not leave me. At night it is just over shadowing my halo. A bit closer to me. A few times it has gotten bigger and bigger.

We have looked above a few other people too. We were curious to find out if the

160

circle of light is over each persons halo. My husband can see a faint circle of light above the halo of some people. We do not see that many people, just family, and we will look more often.

Yesterday, I could feel something powerful, above my head. A different energy, that I have not felt before. I hurried to my husband and asked him to look above me.

He said that the circle of the Holy Spirit as the Dove, was lowering. It had connected to my halo! I could feel the difference!

So I asked, "Is the Holy Spirit to come down, closer, and be in me?" I asked it out loud and asked my husband to ask it out loud, in prayer, to the Lord!

He touched my head and the "Touch" revealed:

"NOT YET   BUT SOON"

By chance I met a very spiritual Rabbi. Very nice teacher and holy man. We just visited and laughed about family and past experiences. After I left and was driving home, I felt as though I had changed? I felt different and light-hearted. Different in my spirit! When I got home, I asked Michael to check my aura, halo and any changes. I could feel a different energy?

What he saw was that my halo had tipped and was a half circle. The Holy Spirit as a dove was resting and lowering into my changed, open to a half circle halo! Michael did a drawing of it immediately! We asked what had happened to me. The answer in the "Touch" revealed:

"A SEGMENT OF YOUR PAST WAS HEALED."

I did feel very free and uplifted for a few hours. But my halo returned to what we think is the normal position and the Holy Spirit moved back to the previous position above the halo. Perhaps I will learn someday how this all works?

Later the "Touch" revealed: "GO TO THE RABBI ASK HIM TO PRAY OVER YOU FOR A SPECIAL BLESSING FROM JEHOVAH GOD THE FATHER."

February 28, 2012 I have tried to talk about the outpouring of the Holy Spirit to Church members, where I attend church. Most times they look at me surprised that I can feel when the Holy Spirit is falling! So I talked to my husband about it. We prayed about it and asked the Lord, "Is anyone at this Church experiencing the Holy Spirit falling and the outpouring?

The "Touch" revealed:

"THOSE WHO LONG FOR IT   AND SEEK IT   WILL RECEIVE IT."

February 29, 2012 Still asking about the Holy Spirit, I wanted to know if there is an outpouring of the Holy Spirit? We talked it over and the "Touch" revealed:

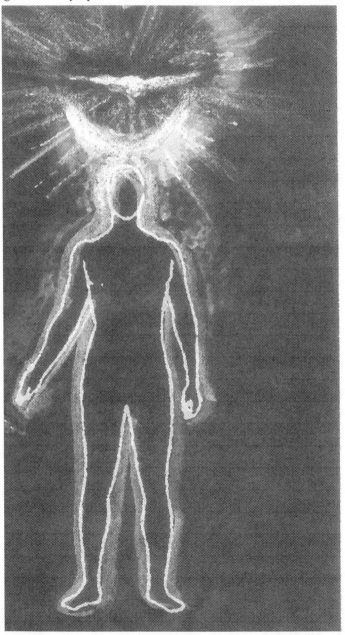

Halo tipped and opened. Holy Spirit moving down to heal a segment of the past.

"THERE IS   THERE WILL BE"

And it did show the pastor of our little church, standing, alone. I suppose that means to only speak to the pastor, while he is alone and in private? I try to avoid him because it is hard to tell him anything. I have only told him about the Holy Spirit falling on the body of believers. Not very much besides that.

I asked again, "Is there anything I should know about the Book? The "Touch" revealed:

"THE HOLY SPIRIT WILL GUIDE YOU."

So that is all that was given. I feel a lot more confidence as I have been corrected. I try not to add my spin on what is revealed. I try to cut it to a shorter answer now. It seems to be a lot smoother as I write.

March 2012 The "Touch" revealed:

"FALSE GUILT"

Of course I try to avoid any correcting or looking into my own deep sub conscience. The wounds of my childhood are understood now. I do not want to ever feel any emotions that are tied up and contained somewhere in my sub conscience. But I do want to learn and improve my spiritual growth. False guilt is a wound in me that causes a lot of anguish. I am aware now, of the wounds I inflicted on my son forty-five years ago. He was just in kindergarten, at the time I became a Christian. Someone hurt him, wounded him and it must have been severe. I feel it was buried and he has no memory of it, as I have no memory of mine. But the Lord does not want me in FALSE GUILT now. So I have tried to understand and study this issue of FALSE GUILT. I have thought and thought about it. Read about it and tried to understand what it is that I am doing wrong?

I went to my husband and explained my concern that I wasn't getting the study on FALSE GUILT.

"Let's pray and ask the Lord to help. This could be a big lesson and I want to finish this book and get it out there in the world". So we agreed and he touched my head. The "Touch" revealed:

"WASTE"

I was confused and said so! "Touch my head again and let's ask what it means. Maybe I am wasting time. Maybe I am wasting money? Maybe it is waste of land after a nuclear accident?" The "Touch" revealed nothing! I have come to know that this means

I am way off track. So I waited a few days. Then I asked my husband if we could talk about it, together, out loud. We talked about the word WASTE and prayed out loud and the "Touch" revealed:

"IT WILL MANIFEST."

I guess that is good? It will show itself. Of course I don't want to waste something. So I prayed and meditated on it and waited a few days. I have a sense of how the answers come now. I try to study, wait, meditate on an issue and then ask. I talked it over with my husband and we asked out loud, again, about waste. The "Touch" revealed:

"WHEN YOU UNDERSTAND."

Well, I was upset. I don't understand what the waste is! And I started complaining a lot about it! Pondering it. It must be important or it would not be shown to me. At the end of this book, means it's a lesson that needs to be known! So I just have to get what it means!

So the next day I asked again. Where is the WASTE? We talked it over and the "Touch" revealed:

"WHEN YOU UNDERSTAND   IT WILL LEAVE."

Oh no! The WASTE is in me! Something will leave me if I can understand! I asked my husband to help me. "Let's ask again, this is critical that I can understand. The Lord knows my insides and knows everything I need to finish the book!" So he touched my head and the "Touch" revealed:

"YOU AND JIMMY ARE THE SAME."

"INJURIES ARE THE SAME."

Oh my God! That is too much for me. I took a few days off and rested. No writing and no searching and no asking! I began to realize the impact of my wounded childhood and being stuck. And to know that my son and I are the same is very painful. I know I can help him walk through the wounds, if I can learn and walk through mine! But after a few days, I wanted the truth and the solution. I have spent these last few years trying to uncover the way to freedom from the childhood wounds. That is why I studied all Paul Hegstrom's material. Everything he had out there. I continue to study all of the Paul Tournier books. I know I am right at the door. So again, I asked out loud about help to understand what is wrong. What is the waste? The "Touch" revealed:

"THE   HELP   WILL   FIND   YOU."

"Ask again! I don't know what to do to find help! Where to go?" And so the

"Touch" revealed:

"YOU WILL UNDERSTAND."

I had to accept it. I can't push when I have an answer. It's best to accept an answer and ponder it for a day or so. The unfolding of an answer is always surprising. So I waited a few days and asked again. The "Touch" revealed:

"STUDY AND UNDERSTAND."

So I began to read and study scripture. Meditate and pray. Relax on this issue of WASTE and wait for the answer to come.

So last Sunday morning I went to church. An early morning Bible study. Small group of about nine people. A very good woman teaching and she's very strong and spirit filled. I like her. She was teaching on II Corinthians 10:4 and I was listening closely. "For the weapons of our warfare are not fleshly but powerful by God for taking down of strongholds"

Well my brain went into block mode! So I stood up and asked if they would talk about that statement. "Let's go over it again?" I asked.

They were kind and polite about it and went one verse before, verse 3 and two verses after, which would be verse 5 and 6. Went over it and over it and my brain would not take it in! Class was over and the leader said we would pick it up next week. I was in shock that my brain was locking up! I have been a Bible scholar all my adult life and this was a first!

So at home I began an in depth study of the three or four verses that were causing my brain to block it. It had to do with "taking captive every thought into the obedience of the Christ".

I knew the wounds of my infancy and as a toddler made it impossible for the word obedience to work for me. There was no room for obedience to anything in order to survive! I was my own ruler. And tearing down strongholds! I wanted someone to lay hands on me! Heal me! And this was saying my warfare! It was my warfare and that I was strong by God! My brain was going in circles!

I had to rest and think about it. In the evening, after praying for all the children and grand children, I asked. "Can we pray about me? Can we ask out loud?, Am I understanding?" The "Touch" revealed:

"CLOSE"

I asked my husband "Please, let me ask one more time? Am I studying in the right

165

direction?" We asked out loud and the "Touch" revealed:

"YES"

Well that is wonderful! I am searching about my biggest lesson? So I started going over and over the scriptures to see which words were related to the WASTE ? Over and over I read. Then I wrote out II Cor. 10: 4- 5 and finally my brain accepted it.

The WASTE is if I do not apply everything that Jesus Christ, The Lamb of God, has done for me. He gave his life so that mine could be saved. So that my sins, my wounds, the affects of the wounds and everything would be covered. I don't have to look for a healer to heal my wounds. The healer is Christ Jesus. The power of God is mine to recognize the symptoms of the wounds as they are triggered or come up. I can choose to recognize a symptom and know it is covered. Then let it go and tell myself, "It's alright. It is only a symptom or a trigger of a memory.

But my brain lock came when the words "bringing every thought into captivity to make it obedient to the Christ".

So I can choose in an instant, when a wounded thought is triggered, that into captivity it goes! In obedience I will give it to Christ. I will live in forgiveness and be sanctified and empowered by all that Jesus gave. I will be free. Everything was given so I could receive the grace to put the wounds under mercy. Under the cross. I will not WASTE all that the Lord did. All is fulfilled and I have got to learn how to live with none of it WASTED!

At night, after praying for all the family, I told my husband what I now understood about "WASTE", and the lesson that the Lord was trying to teach me. I said, "I think I've got it! Let's ask the Lord out loud if I got the lesson right?"

And so we talked it over and asked. The "Touch" revealed:

"WHY DID IT TAKE YOU SO LONG."

I have no answer to give. Perhaps the wounds? Perhaps my stubbornness. Perhaps resistance to change or obedience This little donkey took a long time to be workable. I am just happy I got the lesson.

I have taken some time away from this book. I am feeling the difference in my spirit regarding healing my wounds. Letting the Lord reach the wounded child. I can almost feel the bits of freedom as I am better and better.

Sometimes I check scriptures on a web site: .... Bible.cc It is a great site and easy to use. I was searching on the broken hearted and captives. I came to Luke 4:18 I read it in Greek, Hebrew and English! All the different translations that I could find, I compared them all. There it was, all the time!

The Lord said, "The Spirit of the Lord is upon me, because he hath anointed me to preach the gospel to the poor: He hath sent me to heal the brokenhearted, to preach deliverance to the captives," and so on.

The poor in spirit. Here is the healing of the wounded child. The mercy of God in Christ! The wounded child sins. The child is lost.

"Lest you come to me as a child" You must go back and get the child in yourself and know that the Lord will heal! All the healing is there! You just have to ask the Lord for help. Search inside yourself and recognize your wounds. Study study and then study more! I'm learning at this late date!

I talked about the content of Luke 4:18 with my husband. I added it and I wanted to know if I was interpreting it correctly? I wanted to put it in the ending of my book. "Let's ask" So my husband and I agreed with what we would ask. He touched my head and the "Touch" revealed:

"I APPROVE."

March 27, 2012 After four weekends of company, we settled down to our routine. My husband and I both gained weight with all the company. I am having symptoms from the radiation to my aorta and surrounding veins. They are like leather from the radiation burns. I think I will be OK, if I am careful about what I eat? My husband checks me daily and he can see when I am in trouble. The aorta gets dark and then I will have a lot of chest pain. I have to rest when it happens.

I asked about Joseph of Arimathea and the line of David as King over Israel. Mary, the mother of Jesus, and the their family. I asked because I had made such a mistake about Joseph of Arimathea. We asked out loud so there would be no mistake. The answer to the "Touch" was:

"RESEARCH"

So I asked again. What should I research? Is it Joseph?

The "Touch" revealed:

"YES   AND   GRAIL"

So I asked again, "Is it about me, or my book? What?"

The "Touch" revealed:

"BOOK"

Again I asked, "My Book?" The "Touch" revealed:

"SCRIPTURES"

So I did research about Joseph of Arimathea. It is thought that he was the brother or Uncle of Mary, the mother of Jesus. He was a disciple, but the secret disciple He was a rich merchant and it is believed that he took many people, and family, away from Jerusalem, after the crucifixion. His daughter married Owain (King of the Silures) ap Beli. That is why the records are still available.

I have gone over the Scriptures pertaining to the Last Supper. Joseph of Arimathea was probably at the last supper. But in secret. This is in Greek and Hebrew.

Mark 14:22 And as they continued eating, He took a loaf, said a blessing, broke it and gave it to them, and said: "Take it, this means my body." 23 And taking a cup, He offered thanks and gave it to them, and they all drank out of it. 24 And He said to them:

"THIS MEANS MY 'BLOOD OF THE COVENANT,' WHICH IS TO BE POURED OUT IN BEHALF OF MANY."

So I asked my husband if we could pray and ask out loud about the Grail and the Holy Spirit? Lets ask if they are connected? So we talked and each of us asked, is the Grail and the Holy Spirit connected? And then he touched my head. The "Touch" revealed:

"CONNECTED"

I needed to know more! And so I asked if the ability to see the face of Christ magnified, was because of lineage? Or why can some see the Face? I asked out loud again. My husband touched my head and the "Touch" revealed:

"GIFT OF LOVE"

I am so moved by the answer. It is more than I could have ever hoped for. A gift from God!

So I said, "What about my lineage? I have my record now, my manifest! I am the 48th great grand daughter of Joseph of Arimathea?" Let's ask! And so my husband touched my head and the "Touch" revealed:

168

"NO MEANING"

Nothing! So, even though it is my manifest, my record, it has no meaning, other than just that. Nothing more. I just needed to be straightened out.

And so I asked, out loud, "Can everybody see the Face of Christ? Can anybody?" We prayed and the "Touch" revealed:

"DUAL LOVE"

I looked it up in my dictionary and it is two persons or things! So I asked again,

"Is it us and you? Prayers? What is it?" And the "Touch" revealed:

"THEIR LOVE"

And so I asked, "Is there anything I should know about the 'Grail' .... anything? Lets ask out loud and pray. This is most important!"

The "Touch" revealed:

"IN REMEMBRANCE OF ME."

I have to hold myself in check when I write about this. I cry inside just knowing He said this. But I had to ask the last question. It's the end and I needed to know the end. The blood is in the cup. It wasn't the cup that was the Holy Grail, it was what was in the cup that is the Holy Grail! So I asked, out loud, "Is the Grail Communion? Is it?"

And the "Touch" revealed:

"YES"

So it's Communion!!! I am thrilled to know! "Is there anything I can say in my book? Is there anything I can write for you?" My husband and I asked out loud, so we would be in agreement. He touched my head and words were shown in the "Touch":

"THAT HE LOVES US ALL."

I cry. There is nothing more. Is it over Lord? Am I done? Is it completed? My husband touched my head. The "Touch" revealed:

"IF YOU ARE PLEASED   FINISH."

Chapter Twenty-Four
Prophecy on Scripture and Understanding

The following information was given over almost a 6 month period of time. In these last 2 chapters the questions and answers have been organized by subject rather than by date. This has been a learning experience. I would study and discuss the information, then when I thought I had enough understanding to properly frame a question I would ask the Lord. Sometimes things can be shown in a vision to Michael and then I have to develop an understanding and then ask a relevant question to that vision, such as the nuclear issue. Sometimes an answer will lead to another question and I have to ask a few more questions to get it straight and understand.

As I write these words this morning Michael and I talked about these last two chapters. We were concerned how they would be perceived. So we asked the Lord, are we prophesying?

The Lord said, "NO".

Then I asked, are we interpreting?

The "Touch" revealed:

"I AM ANSWERING YOUR QUESTIONS"

So that is how it works. I study and study. A question will come to mind and I talk with Michael about it. Time will pass and then we ask.

I asked out loud, carefully, "Do you want me to write anything, Lord?" Michael touched my head and the "Touch" revealed:

"YOUR MANIFEST BELONGS TO YOU AS IT IS WRITTEN"

I sat down very close to Michael.

"I want to ask about India. At the end of July 2012, the power outage affected 600 to 700 million people. Let me pray and ask out loud."

"The power outage in India, is that how the 'severe nuclear accident' happens?"

Michael touched my head and the "Touch" revealed:

"NOT THIS TIME"

(India should fix it's infrastructure and not pursue a space program. Perhaps this accident would not come to pass? My will be done and they will be done. This means free will).

"This severe nuclear accident, is it the 'beginning of birth pains' of Matthew 24:8 ?" The "Touch" revealed:

"COULD BE
THERE COULD BE MORE NUCLEAR ACCIDENTS
BUT ONE IN INDIA COULD BE MORE SEVERE

IT DEPENDS ON
IF MAN'S CAPABLE OF PREVENTING"

CAUSE AND EFFECT"

It is up to man to stop this dangerous path. Start now to prevent the accidents that could come to be. I will not ask any more questions about nuclear problems.

"The face of God in the Old Testament that David saw, and the face my son Jimmy and I saw, is it the same face that Jesus said 'If you can see me you have seen the Father?'" The "Touch" revealed:

"YES THE FACE OF A LOVING GOD"

I asked, "The face of God that my son Jimmy, Eurieni and I saw, can sinners see?" The "Touch" revealed:

"IF I WANT THEM"

I asked, "Can I pray over my son Jimmy? Can I anoint him with oil and pray over him?" The "Touch" revealed:

"YOU BELONG TO ME AND YOU HAVE THE POWER"

I have had people involved with this book say that I am just dealing with a spirit! I know better. But to confirm to the world, I said, "Are you The Son of God, The Lord Jesus Christ, The Savior, The Lamb of God?" The "Touch" revealed:

"YES"

"Are the Father, The Son and The Holy Spirit, One?" The "Touch" revealed:

"YES   YOUR MIND CAN NOT COMPREHEND"

I asked, "Is the Ark, the Bread, Oil and Lamb received in the Old Testament the same as the New Testament? The Lamb of God, Bread of Life and the Anointing Oil of the Holy Spirit?" The "Touch" revealed:

"YOU ARE LEARNING"

I asked, "Will the Shekinah Glory not spare life?" The "Touch" revealed:

"ACCEPT AND BE BAPTISED"

I asked, "Is the Glory Light, Shekinah Light and Glory Light Circle around the Holy Spirit as a Dove, all the same Glory Light from You!?" The "Touch" revealed:

"YES"

I could not understand Genesis 1:27 God Elohim created man and woman. He created male and female. But then over in Genesis 2:7 Yahweh Elohim created Ha dam or Adam of dust and breathed into his nostrils, the breath. And man became living, Hay yah. "What is this Lord? Is it a separate people?"

Is Adam different from creating man and woman over in Genesis 1:27?"

"THE FIRST JEW"

I asked, "Was there time between creating the first man and woman in Genesis

1:27 and creating Adam, the first Jew. Did time pass?" The "Touch" revealed:

"A WHILE"

I asked, "Did Eve go into the center of the garden to the tree to worship?" The "Touch" revealed:

"DO NOT GO INTO THE GROVE OR DO NOT PARTAKE OF FRUIT OF THE TREE"

I asked, "The Nephilim, were they a separate race of men? Were they giants?" The "Touch" revealed:

"FALLEN ANGELS"

I asked, "Are their DNA in humans today?" The "Touch" revealed:

"BRED DOWN"

I asked, "Did some live on?" The "Touch" revealed:

"AFTER THE FLOOD NOAH AND HIS FAMILY HAD SOME"

I asked, "During the flood, did other peoples live on earth and survive besides Noah's family group?" The "Touch" revealed:

"MOST LIKELY"

I asked, "At the time that you created the first Jew—Ha Adam and Eve—were there a great many people on the earth?" And the "Touch" revealed:

"NOT THAT MANY"

I asked, "With the nephilim DNA in man, does it matter today? Does it matter spiritually? Is there a difference between men? In their understanding or believing in God?" The "Touch" revealed:

"MINUTE"

I asked, "Lord, you said that Satan was a fallen angel. He was a nephilim. The nephilim took wives from among the daughters of men. Is this where the people began to worship Satan? Which is the Old Testament beginning of the worship of other gods?"

"HALLELUJAH   YOU GOT IT RIGHT"

"I want to ask about Joseph now. Joseph wrestled the angel. He overcame himself? Joseph overcame man? He wrestled himself?" The "Touch" revealed:

"YES HE DIDN'T EXPECT IT BUT IT HAPPENED"

I said, "Joseph succeeded! He experienced God? Jumped in to know God!" The "Touch" revealed:

"YES IF YOU JUMP IN THE WATER WILL YOU BE WET"

I asked, "Is the Pineal experience of Joseph guarded for good only?" The "Touch" revealed:

"IF YOU SEEK GOOD OR EVIL YOU HAVE FREE WILL"

I asked, "When you told Eve she would be the mother of many nations, did you mean the Jews?" The "Touch" revealed:

"YES   OF MANY SEED"

I asked, "In Genesis 4:6 why wasn't Cain's offering accepted?" The "Touch" revealed:

"KNEW HIS SPIRIT"

I asked, "If a Jew, is there anything we need to observe?" The "Touch" revealed:

"CHANGE WAS BAPTISMAL   AND TO BE BORN AGAIN"

"Is there anything I should know about Jewish Temple worship? The blood sacrifice in the temple to cover man's sin? I don't understand it all?" The "Touch" revealed:

"THE BLOOD WORSHIP STOPPED ON THE CROSS"

I asked, "Lord, when you die or pass on, is it to be with you? Resting in the Lord, or sleep? What is it?" The 'touch' revealed:

"DIMENSION"

"Is the lost soul into nothingness, separation, that I experienced twice, is there mercy?" The "Touch" revealed:

"ITS UP TO ME"

There is a lot said about the Catholics. So I asked. "What about the Catholic

Church. Is it 'The Harlot or the false religion in the Bible'?" The "Touch" revealed:

"NO"

"Can those within the Catholic church be saved and belong to you, Lord?" The "Touch" revealed:

"FOLLOW THE TEN COMMANDMENTS
LOVE THE LORD
BELIEVE
BELIEF AND FAITH
BE BAPTISED"

I asked the Lord, out loud, " 'As it was in the time of Noah, so will it be with the coming of the Son of Man.' Luke 17:26. Does that mean there will be few people left on earth?" The "Touch" revealed:

"HAVE YOU HEARD OF THE RAPTURE"

Sometimes my questions do not make perfect sense? I did not study far enough in Luke 17: It clearly is the rapture. So I asked again, "Lord, so the coming of the Son of Man is after the rapture?" The "Touch" revealed:

"YES"

"In the end, will the land be able to be given back?" The "Touch" revealed:

"I WILL BE THERE"

"In the Old Testament Joel 2:3 the armies come up against Israel. They come upon the blossoming land, like the Garden of Eden. Fire leaves a wasteland behind them as the armies pass through. Is this what happens in the war to come at the battle of Armageddon?"

"YES"

I asked, "Why can't we help, with healing? Is it a ministry? Can anyone heal? How does it work?" The "Touch" revealed:

"THE CHOSEN"

"Who are those that have the circle of light of the Holy Spirit as a Dove above their halo? Over themselves?" The "Touch" revealed:

"ARE HEARTWORTHY"

"Do they have to believe in you, Lord?" The "Touch" revealed:

"CHRISTIANS"

Michael and I got into a debate about everyone having a halo. He said that he could not see the halo above everyone. So we prayed about it and I asked out loud, "Lord Jesus, does everyone have a halo?"

The "Touch" revealed:

"YES   NOT ALL ARE VISIBLE"

"What makes a halo visible?" I asked. The "Touch" revealed:

"LOVE FOR ANOTHER HUMAN"

I asked out loud, "Is the Kingdom of Heaven within you or along side?" The "Touch" revealed:

"AMOUNGST YOU   BESIDE YOU   WITHIN YOU
HOW YOU INTERPRET"

Chapter Twenty-Five

Revealings on Healing and The End

While my journey in writing this book has given me understanding of the different paths to healing of the wounds in childhood, the revealings by the 'touch' from the Lord are very specific. I do believe in counseling and therapy. Professional help and guidance can give the wounded and searching soul the way of help. I still study and read Paul Tournier and many others, as much as I can find the time.

The intimate details of my early years were a message of a child's wounds. The revealings that would be taught by the 'touch' do not contradict counseling and therapy in any way. Meditation is very important for healing. We were shown that after a very strong prayer time and then a meditation period of time, in my aura and spirit I was a very tiny little girl.

When we asked, "why would I turn into a child in my spirit?" The "Touch" revealed:

"TO REMEMBER YOUR INJURIES"

I asked, "Am I interpreting this right?" The "Touch" revealed:

"IN YOUR CASE"

So it is different for everyone. During and after this meditation and prayer time, I did not have conscious memories or remember any incidents from my childhood. But

179

perhaps in my spirit I was healing?

I have learned a great deal about fear and confusion caused by wounds to the child or the young. I have learned from the revealings of the "Touch", as the days go by, and more is written down. Perhaps you will understand this healing message and prepare your heart. What is said in this book is not only for me, it is for you as well. There is no difference between the meanings in the 'touch' for you or for me!

We were asked, by the Lord, to pray over a person. We asked "why" and what was the reason for the request? Michael and I did not understand. The "Touch" revealed:

"FAVOR"

While still confused, I asked Michael, "Is it a favor for me, or the person themselves or their family? Who is the favor for?" The "Touch" revealed:

"FOR THE FATHER"

We were surprised at the answer and that it was for Jehovah God the Father! So again we asked, out loud, "Are we praying and asking for an anointing?" The "Touch" revealed:

"CLEANSING HIS SPIRIT"

Of course we did pray for the person, but I needed to know more. So I asked, "Does a demon spirit come from the outside to inside of a person?" The "Touch" revealed:

"YES"

I asked, "Does an unclean spirit come from the inside? Is it willing participation and the unclean spirit comes from the inside?" The "Touch" revealed:

"YES"

I asked, "Does the reading of the word of God, cast out unclean spirits?" The "Touch" revealed:

"TAKES MORE"

"Does it take an anointed person?" I asked. The "Touch" revealed:

"SOMETIMES"

"What is God's preferred way to cast out unclean spirit?" The "Touch" revealed:

180

"CHANGE OF HEART   SINCERITY   LOVE"

"Can I take communion all by myself?" The "Touch" revealed:

"IF YOU HAVE BEEN BAPTIZED"

"Do you mean baptized by immersion?" The "Touch" revealed:

"PREFERABLY"

"How can I do better? How can I become not so vulnerable to warfare and the enemy onslaught?" The "Touch" revealed:

"KEEP LOVE IN YOUR HEART"

"For you Lord?" I asked. The "Touch" revealed:

"YES AND MAN"

Sometimes the teaching in the Book of Acts. Mentions not receiving the Holy Spirit. This is because of doing something wrong or misunderstanding.

So I asked, out loud, to Michael, "Am I doing something wrong?" The "Touch" revealed:

"DRAWING CONCLUSIONS"

Well, of course I was upset. So I asked, "How can I change my brain?" The "Touch" revealed:

"ON YOUR KNEES"

After calming down, praying and thinking about willing to change and grow, I asked, "Is my drawing conclusions from my infant and childhood wounds? I'm going to solve it! I will fix it. I am in control. I'm going to protect myself. I'm on my own! I can't trust anyone. I won't trust anyone. Not even the Lord." The "Touch" revealed:

"VERY GOOD"

So over the next few months, the Lord showed through the 'touch' the way the wounds are finally healed. I am just learning it and praying and meditating on this way the Lord wants.

I asked, "Why do I dream, once in a while, such a terrifying dream? A terror? Similar to the injuries when I was a baby or toddler?" The "Touch" revealed:

"LIKE A FISH FROM THE SEA"

And it showed a picture of a calm sea and a fish popped up out of the water. So I asked again if it was the wound, just in my sub conscious, breaking through like a fish from the sea. The "Touch" revealed:

"YES'

I forgot about it. I didn't think it was a teaching from the Lord or something to ask about. A few weeks passed. As I was getting ready for sleep one night, my head on the pillow, Michael looked at me. With his eyes closed he saw a huge golden fish! It had jumped out of the water and was golden! I knew what it was! A wound had been transformed! Romans 8:28 All things work together for good for those who love God. The Holy Spirit is as a golden glory Light. Earlier in this book I explained the Glory Light. So I asked the Lord, to be sure I was interpreting this correctly. "When you consciously give a wound or injury over to the Lord, and Holy Spirit, then it is transformed into Gold! The healing takes place and is transformed!" The "Touch" revealed:

"RIGHT"

"So I finally figured it out. These are the steps for the wounds as a child, in the sub-conscious. It starts with a softened heart. In prayer, you soften your heart, humbly soften. You give the wound to Jehovah God the Father, in the Name of Jesus Christ the Son and the Holy Spirit of God will transform the wound to Golden light of His Glory! Is this right Lord?"

"GOOD"

The affects of the wounds will not be the same for you, if you are triggered. You become aware slowly, that you are not at the mercy of your response to a trigger. You have a new control and peace. I realize that it is in obedience and a softened heart that you give it over to God. But it works!

"Lord, we are not in the time of the four horsemen yet. That is of the end time. That has not begun and is in the future time." The 'touch' revealed.

"YES"

"Lord, there will be no invasion of Israel until the battle of Armageddon."

"YES"

"The United States is not mentioned in the End Time. What about the United States of America? The "Touch" revealed:

"ITS UP TO THE PEOPLE"

"Do you mean repent, turn around and pray?" The "Touch" revealed:

"BELIEVING IN THE FATHER   THE SON   THE HOLY SPIRIT LOVING THY GOD"

I was told that in the future it would be revealed about the ten nations, the mystery Babylon and mystery of Revelation 17. The nations have not formed and come together as they will in the future.

The "Touch" revealed:

"YOUR JOURNEY IN THE BOOK IS TO UNDERSTAND.   PREPARE THEIR HEART   AND THOUGHT   FOR WHAT COULD OCCUR AND WILL OCCUR"

And so I asked, "If they trust me, as I've told the truth, they will know to turn toward You as we move into what will occur." The "Touch" revealed:

"YES"

The Lord kept revealing the words fear and preparation. So Michael and I talked about it and discussed it. Then I asked out loud, "Lord what is fear and preparation?" Michael touched my head. The "Touch" revealed:

"FEAR AND PREPARATION IN THE BOOK"

So Michael and I were really confused. Are we supposed to be in preparation for problems? What are we to prepare? We talked it over. What are we to prepare for? Michael touched my head and the "Touch" revealed:

"MY COMING"

We both started to cry a little. I said to Michael, "We better ask how can we prepare?"
Michael touched my head and the "Touch" revealed:

"REJOICE"

Epilogue

In the last six months Michael and I have learned a great deal about the future. It is all revealed the same way. I ask a question of the Lord, out loud. Michael and I talk it over and sort out the details. No mistakes, if we can help it. I ask the question. Michael 'touches' my head. The answer from the Lord is spelled out to Michael. Clearly. If there is any confusion, I ask again. There are times that I have asked a question that is not going to be answered. Something that we should not know. Should not be asked. Then there is no response and Michael sees nothing. His eyes are always closed as he waits on the Lord.

Because man has free will, the time line of the future events seem open. Somewhat undetermined. This is clarified more at the end of this chapter. I can only gauge or estimate by my age and if I was told I would experience what is going to occur.

The Fukushima issue will be contained. There will be a nuclear accident in India caused by an electrical infrastructure failure.

These are the pertinent questions I have asked on the end times.

"Lord, will Michael and I be in the 'Last Generation' of the end times?" The 'touch' revealed,

NO

"What is a generation then, Lord?" The 'touch' revealed,

BIRTH TO DEATH

"Are my children of the Last Generation, Lord?" The 'touch' revealed,

YES   AS IT STANDS NOW

Michael's children were born starting around 1956. So this I believe is the approximate life span time or birth period of the 'Last Generation'.

"Lord, can I still be here for the Rapture?" The 'touch' revealed,

NOT IN YOUR GENERATION

"Lord, we hear a lot about an EMP, electromagnetic pulse. Is that what will occur in the United States?" The 'touch' revealed,

CAN NOT   WILL NOT

"In scripture, before the Great Tribulation, there is a time called 'the beginning of birth pains'. Is that the hard times ahead, Lord?" The 'touch' revealed,

LIVE AS 150 YEARS AGO   KNOWLEDGE

"Is this caused by a combination of the manipulated seeds dying, then causing loss of food production and failing economics, Lord?" The 'touch' revealed,

COVER ALL ASPECTS

"Will living as 150 years ago be without electricity, Lord?" The 'touch' revealed,

IT CAN BE

"What forces us to lead into living as 150 years ago? Is it a financial issue, Lord?"

NO

"To live as 150 years ago, is it brought about quickly, Lord?" The 'touch' revealed,

FAST ENOUGH

"Is this time brought on by a disaster, Lord?" The 'touch' revealed,

MOST LIKELY

"As a disaster happens in the future, it starts a chain of events? A demand on food supply? Is it then that the food shortages happen? Is the chain of events causing us to live as a 150 years ago setting, Lord?" The 'touch' revealed,

CONFLICT

"Will the conflict encompass U.S., Mexico and Canada, Lord?" The 'touch' revealed,

CAN BE LIMITED

(I understand this to mean, only the United States.)

"Is this an accident or a terrorist strike inside America, Lord?" The 'touch' revealed,

COULD BE

"Do we have some time to learn the knowledge of how to prepare? Some time or years, Lord?" The 'touch' revealed,

YOU   HAVE   TIME

"Is the time of living as 150 years ago, before the 7 year 'great tribulation', Lord?" 'touch' revealed,

YES

"Will Michael and I experience living as 150 years ago, Lord?" 'touch' revealed,

SOME

"So why am I learning to live as 150 years ago, if I won't be here, Lord?" 'touch' revealed,

BE HELPING PEOPLE IN GREAT TRIBULATION AFTER THE RAPTURE

"Will people that live through the 'Great Tribulation' live on into the millennium reign of Christ, Lord?"

YES

"Will people accept Christ during the millennium reign of Christ as Messiah, Lord?" 'touch' revealed

NOT ALL

"Lord, those that live through the 'Great Tribulation', will they live the 1000 years, through the millennial reign of Christ?" The 'touch revealed,

NO

"Who is it that will live on earth with those that live through the tribulation time? Will they be the children born to people left on earth, Lord?" The 'touch' revealed,

CHOSEN

"Can I write about all of this Lord?" The 'touch' revealed,

EXAMPLES

"What examples Lord? The things that I know?" The 'touch' revealed,

ITS HAPPENING   WRITE ABOUT IT   EXPLAIN
YOURSELF

"Do you mean explain my feelings about people Lord?" The 'touch' revealed,

THE REASON

"I still don't understand what is the reason Lord?" Michael 'touched' my head and saw,

THEY ARE SUPPOSED TO DO WHAT YOU ARE DOING NOW

So here are some of the things we are doing now, to prepare. We study the book, 'SEED TO SEED' by Suzanne Ashworth. We can now grow vegetables and save seed for the next season. The powers that be, are trying to prevent germination of any food that is grown. It is called 'The Terminator' or the 'Neutron Bomb of Agriculture. It's greed based. Since 2006 the honey bee population began to die out from pesticides. Now around 70% of bee populations have died as a result of Colony Collapse Disorder. This will contribute to the end time food shortages. So we plant honey bee friendly plants.

We also planted fruit trees and berry vines. We are learning to can and preserve by watching you tube and use the 'BALL' canning book. Things that you can do, is to have a supply of dehydrated food set aside, have a small greenhouse with potted plants, have dwarf fruit trees inside, in sunny window area. We are composting everything in the worm factory and vermicompost for castings and liquid fertilizer.

Get the book, 'Back to Basics' on eBay, a world of information. It's trial and error, hands on learning! Potted plants in windows, on balconies, back yards and small spaces. Buy dwarf fruit trees and experiment. Study and experiment with different plants and small greenhouse.

So Michael and I talked it over again, the living as 150 years ago.

Then we asked, "Is living as 150 years ago and as a prepper, being self-reliant, caused by the nuclear accident in India or the conflict in America? Which is first Lord?"

DEPENDS ON MAN

"Lord, the conflict in America, that puts us back to 150 years ago, is it before the rapture?" Michael 'touch' my head and saw,

UNDETERMINED

REVELATION NOT ETCHED IN STONE

LIKE THE SUN RISE

AND THE SUN SET

THE COLORS CHANGE IN YOUR DIMENSION

"Does the 'free will' of man play a part, or is relevant, in the 'undetermined' revelation of destiny Lord?" Michael 'touched' my head and saw,

FREE WILL HAS A BEARING ON IT

"Does the coming conflict within the United States, cause all to live as 150 years ago, Lord?" Michael 'touched' my head and saw,

AS IT PROGRESSES

MORE THAN ONE CONFLICT

"Will I be here for this conflict, Lord?" Michael 'touched' my head and saw,

IT DEPENDS ON UNDETERMINED SITUATIONS

"Living as 150 years ago, is it the 'beginning of birth pains' Lord?" Michael 'touched' my head and saw

TRIBULATION

"Lord, does God answer our prayers as we pray for the hearts of our family and loved ones, to turn toward you?" Michael 'touched' my head and saw,

HEART WARNING TIME

END

RAPTURE

IT WILL BE TIME FOR THE SIGNS

"Beginning of 'birth pains' in scripture, is there anything I should know, to tell or write about, Lord?" Michael 'touched' my head and saw,

IT WILL BE EVIDENT

So, this is the time of the HEART WARNING TIME. There is time and then will be the 'signs'. All the signs will be 'EVIDENT'. Know the signs. Prepare.